RECAST VAT DIRECTIVE

Copyright © 2014 TaxEye

The text in this book is of unofficial nature. The authors, publisher and any other person involved in preparing, publishing or selling this book are not responsible for the results of any actions taken on the basis of the information contained in it nor for any errors or omissions contained therein.

ISBN-13: 978-1497551121
ISBN-10: 1497551129

TABLE OF CONTENTS

TABLE OF CONTENTS 3
TITLE I - SUBJECT MATTER AND SCOPE 7
TITLE II - TERRITORIAL SCOPE 10
TITLE III - TAXABLE PERSONS 11
TITLE IV - TAXABLE TRANSACTIONS 13
    Chapter 1 Supply of Goods 13
    Chapter 2 Intra-Community Acquisition of Goods 16
    Chapter 3 Supply of Services 17
    Chapter 4 Importation of Goods 18
TITLE V - PLACE OF TAXABLE TRANSACTIONS 19
    Chapter 1 Place of Supply of Goods 19
        Section 1: Supply of Goods without Transport 19
        Section 2: Supply of Goods with Transport 19
        Section 3: Supply of goods on board ships, aircraft or trains 21
        Section 4: Supplies of gas through a natural gas system, of electricity and of heat or cooling energy through heating and cooling networks 22
    Chapter 2 Place of an Intra-Community Acquisition of Goods 23
    Chapter 3 Place of Supply of Services 24
        Section 1: Definitions 24
        Section 2: General rules 24
        Section 3: Particular provisions 25
            Subsection 1: Supply of services by intermediaries 25
            Subsection 2: Supply of services connected with immovable property 25
            Subsection 3: Supply of transport 25
            Subsection 4: Supply of cultural, artistic, sporting, scientific, educational, entertainment and similar services, ancillary transport services and valuations of and work on movable property 26
            Subsection 5: Supply of restaurant and catering services 26
            Subsection 6: Hiring of means of transport 27
            Subsection 7: Supply of restaurant and catering services for consumption on board ships, aircraft or trains 27
            Subsection 8: Supply of electronic services to non-taxable persons 28
            Subsection 9: Supply of services to non-taxable persons outside the Community 28
            Subsection 10: Prevention of double taxation or non-taxation 29
    Chapter 4 Place of Importation of Goods 30
TITLE VI - CHARGEABLE EVENT AND CHARGEABILITY OF VAT 31
    Chapter 1 General Provisions 31
    Chapter 2 Supply of Goods or Services 31
    Chapter 3 Intra-Community Acquisition of Goods 32
    Chapter 4 Importation of Goods 33
TITLE VII - TAXABLE AMOUNT 34
    Chapter 1 Definition 34
    Chapter 2 Supply of Goods or Services 35
    Chapter 3 Intra-Community Acquisition of Goods 38

Chapter 4 Importation of Goods 39
Chapter 5 Miscellaneous Provisions 40
TITLE VIII - RATES 41
Chapter 1 Application of Rates 41
Chapter 2 Structure and level of Rates 42
   Section 1: Standard Rate 42
   Section 2: Reduced Rates 42
   Section 3: Particular Provisions 43
Chapter 3 44
Chapter 4 Special Provisions applying until the Adoption of Definitive Arrangements 45
Chapter 5 Temporary Provisions 48
TITLE IX - EXEMPTIONS 50
Chapter 1 General Provisions 50
Chapter 2 Exemptions for Certain Activities in the Public Interest 51
Chapter 3 Exemptions for other Activities 54
Chapter 4 Exemptions for Intra-Community Transactions 56
   Section 1: Exemptions related to the Supply of Goods 56
   Section 2 Exemptions for Intra-Community Acquisitions of Goods 57
   Section 3 Exemptions for Certain Transport Services 58
Chapter 5: Exemptions on Importation 59
Chapter 6 Exemptions on Exportation 62
Chapter 7 Exemptions Related to International Transport 64
Chapter 8 Exemptions Relating to Certain Transactions treated as Exports 65
Chapter 9 Exemptions for the Supply of Services by Intermediaries 66
Chapter 10 Exemptions for Transactions relating to International Trade 66
   Section 1: Customs warehouses, warehouses other than customs warehouses and similar arrangements 66
   Section 2: Transactions exempted with a view to export and in the framework of trade between the Member States 69
   Section 3: Provisions common to Sections 1 and 2 69
TITLE X DEDUCTIONS 70
Chapter 1 Origin and Scope of Right of Deduction 70
Chapter 2 Proportional Deduction 73
Chapter 3 Restrictions on the Right of Deduction 75
Chapter 4 Rules Governing Exercise of the Right of Deduction 76
Chapter 5 Adjustment of Deductions 78
TITLE XI - OBLIGATIONS OF TAXABLE PERSONS AND CERTAIN NON-TAXABLE PERSONS 81
Chapter 1 Obligation to Pay 81
   Section 1 Persons liable for payment of VAT to the tax authorities 81
   Section 2: Payment arrangements 87
Chapter 2 Identification 89
Chapter 3 Invoicing 91
   Section 1: Definition 91
   Section 2: Concept of invoice 91
   Section 3: Issue of invoices 91
   Section 4: Content of invoices 94
   Section 5: Paper invoices and electronic invoices 97
   Section 6: Simplification measures 98
Chapter 4 Accounting 100

- Section 1: Definition 100
- Section 2: General obligations 100
- Section 3: Specific obligations relating to the storage of all invoices 100
- Section 4: Right of access to invoices stored by electronic means in another Member State 102
- Chapter 5 Returns 103
- Chapter 6 Recapitulative Statements 106
- Chapter 7 Miscellaneous Provisions 110
- Chapter 8 Obligations Relating to Certain Importations and Exportations 111
  - Section 1: Importation 111
  - Section 2: Exportation 111

TITLE XII - SPECIAL SCHEMES 113
- Chapter 1 Special Scheme for Small Enterprises 113
  - Section 1: Simplified procedures for charging and collection 113
  - Section 2: Exemptions or graduated relief 113
  - Section 3: Reporting and review 116
- Chapter 2 Common Flat-Rate Scheme for Farmers 117
- Chapter 3 Special Scheme for Travel Agents 121
- Chapter 4 Special Arrangements for Second-Hand Goods, Works of Art, Collectors' Items and Antiques 123
  - Section 1: Definitions 123
  - Section 2: Special arrangements for taxable dealers 124
    - Subsection 1: Margin scheme 124
    - Subsection 2: Transitional arrangements for second-hand means of transport .127
  - Section 3: Special arrangements for sales by public auction 129
  - Section 4: Measures to prevent distortion of competition and tax evasion 131
- Chapter 5 Special Scheme for Investment Gold 132
  - Section 1: General provisions 132
  - Section 2: Exemption from VAT 132
  - Section 3: Taxation option 133
  - Section 4: Transactions on a regulated gold bullion market 133
  - Section 5: Special rights and obligations for traders in investment gold 134
- Chapter 6 Special Scheme for Non-Established Taxable Persons supplying Electronic Services to Non-Taxable Persons 136
  - Section 1: General provisions 136
  - Section 2: Special scheme for electronically supplied services 136

TITLE XIII DEROGATIONS 140
- Chapter 1 Derogations Applying Until the Adoption of Definitive Arrangements 140
  - Section 1: Derogations for States which were members of the Community on 1 January 1978 140
  - Section 2: Derogations for States which acceded to the Community after 1 January 1978 141
  - Section 3: Provisions common to Sections 1 and 2 144
- Chapter 2 Derogations Subject to Authorization 146
  - Section 1: Simplification measures and measures to prevent tax evasion or avoidance 146
  - Section 2: International Agreements 147

TITLE XIV - MISCELLANEOUS 148
- Chapter 1 Implementing Measures 148
- Chapter 2 VAT Committee 148
- Chapter 3 Conversion Rates 148

Chapter 4 Other Taxes, Duties and Charges 149
TITLE XV - FINAL PROVISIONS 150
    Chapter 1 Transitional Arrangements for the Taxation of Trade between Member States 150
    Chapter 2 Transitional Measures applicable in the Context of Accession to the European Union 151
    Chapter 3 Transposition and Entry Into Force 154
ANNEX I 155
ANNEX II 155
ANNEX III 156
ANNEX IV 157
ANNEX V 158
ANNEX VI 159
ANNEX VII 159
ANNEX VIII 160
ANNEX IX 160
ANNEX X 162
ANNEX XI 164
ANNEX XII 166
VAT E-CONSULTANT APP 196

Title I - Subject Matter and Scope

Article 1

1. This Directive establishes the common system of value added tax (VAT).

2. The principle of the common system of VAT entails the application to goods and services of a general tax on consumption exactly proportional to the price of the goods and services, however many transactions take place in the production and distribution process before the stage at which the tax is charged.

On each transaction, VAT, calculated on the price of the goods or services at the rate applicable to such goods or services, shall be chargeable after deduction of the amount of VAT borne directly by the various cost components.

The common system of VAT shall be applied up to and including the retail trade stage.

Article 2

1. The following transactions shall be subject to VAT:

   (a) the supply of goods for consideration within the territory of a Member State by a taxable person acting as such;

   (b) the intra-Community acquisition of goods for consideration within the territory of a Member State by:

   (i) a taxable person acting as such, or a non-taxable legal person, where the vendor is a taxable person acting as such who is not eligible for the exemption for small enterprises provided for in Articles 282 to 292 and who is not covered by Articles 33 or 36;

   (ii) in the case of new means of transport, a taxable person, or a non-taxable legal person, whose other acquisitions are not subject to VAT pursuant to Article 3(1), or any other non-taxable person;

   (iii) in the case of products subject to excise duty, where the excise duty on the intra-Community acquisition is chargeable, pursuant to Directive 92/12/EEC, within the territory of the Member State, a taxable person, or a non-taxable legal person, whose other acquisitions are not subject to VAT pursuant to Article 3(1);

   (c) the supply of services for consideration within the territory of a Member State by a taxable person acting as such;

   (d) the importation of goods.

2.

(a) For the purposes of point of paragraph 1(b), the following shall be regarded as "means of transport", where they are intended for the transport of persons or goods:

    (i) motorized land vehicles the capacity of which exceeds 48 cubic centimeters or the power of which exceeds 7,2 kilowatts;

    (ii) vessels exceeding 7,5 meters in length, with the exception of vessels used for navigation on the high seas and carrying passengers for reward, and of vessels used for the purposes of commercial, industrial or fishing activities, or for rescue or assistance at sea, or for inshore fishing;

    (iii) aircraft the take-off weight of which exceeds 1550 kilograms, with the exception of aircraft used by airlines operating for reward chiefly on international routes.

(b) These means of transport shall be regarded as "new" in the cases:

    (i) of motorized land vehicles, where the supply takes place within six months of the date of first entry into service or where the vehicle has travelled for no more than 6000 kilometers;

    (ii) of vessels, where the supply takes place within three months of the date of first entry into service or where the vessel has sailed for no more than 100 hours;

    (iii) of aircraft, where the supply takes place within three months of the date of first entry into service or where the aircraft has flown for no more than 40 hours.

(c) Member States shall lay down the conditions under which the facts referred to in point (b) may be regarded as established.

3. Products subject to excise duty" shall mean energy products, alcohol and alcoholic beverages and manufactured tobacco, as defined by current Community legislation, but not gas supplied through a natural gas system situated within the territory of the Community or any network connected to such a system".

Article 3

1. By way of derogation from Article 2(1)(b)(i), the following transactions shall not be subject to VAT:

(a) the intra-Community acquisition of goods by a taxable person or a non-taxable legal person, where the supply of such goods within the territory of the Member State of acquisition would be exempt pursuant to Articles 148 and 151;

(b) the intra-Community acquisition of goods, other than those referred to in point (a) and Article 4, and other than new means of transport or products subject to excise duty, by a taxable person for the purposes of his agricultural, forestry or fisheries business subject to the common flat-rate scheme for farmers, or by a taxable person who carries out only supplies of goods or services in respect of which VAT is not deductible, or by a non-taxable legal person.

2. Point (b) of paragraph 1 shall apply only if the following conditions are met:

 (a) during the current calendar year, the total value of intra-Community acquisitions of goods does not exceed a threshold which the Member States shall determine but which may not be less than EUR 10,000 or the equivalent in national currency;

 (b) during the previous calendar year, the total value of intra-Community acquisitions of goods did not exceed the threshold provided for in point (a).

The threshold which serves as the reference shall consist of the total value, exclusive of VAT due or paid in the Member State in which dispatch or transport of the goods began, of the intra-Community acquisitions of goods as referred to under point (b) of paragraph 1.

3. Member States shall grant taxable persons and non-taxable legal persons eligible under point (b) of paragraph 1 the right to opt for the general scheme provided for in Article 2(1)(b)(i).

Member States shall lay down the detailed rules for the exercise of the option referred to in the first subparagraph, which shall in any event cover a period of two calendar years.

Article 4

In addition to the transactions referred to in Article 3, the following transactions shall not be subject to VAT:

 (a) the intra-Community acquisition of second-hand goods, works of art, collectors' items or antiques, as defined in points (1) to (4) of Article 311(1), where the vendor is a taxable dealer acting as such and VAT has been applied to the goods in the Member State in which their dispatch or transport began, in accordance with the margin scheme provided for in Articles 312 to 325;

 (b) the intra-Community acquisition of second-hand means of transport, as defined in Article 327(3), where the vendor is a taxable dealer acting as such and VAT has been applied to the means of transport in the Member State in which their dispatch or transport began, in accordance with the transitional arrangements for second-hand means of transport;

 (c) the intra-Community acquisition of second-hand goods, works of art, collectors' items or antiques, as defined in points (1) to (4) of Article 311(1), where the vendor is an organizer of sales by public auction, acting as such, and VAT has been applied to the goods in the Member State in which their dispatch or transport began, in accordance with the special arrangements for sales by public auction.

Title II - Territorial Scope

Article 5

1. For the purposes of applying this Directive, the following definitions shall apply:

    (a) "Community" and "territory of the Community" mean the territories of the Member States as defined in point (2);

    (b) "Member State" and "territory of a Member State" mean the territory of each Member State of the Community to which the Treaty establishing the European Community is applicable, in accordance with Article 299 of that Treaty, with the exception of any territory referred to in Article 6 of this Directive;

    (c) "third territories" means those territories referred to in Article 6;

    (d) "third country" means any State or territory to which the Treaty is not applicable.

Article 6

1. This Directive shall not apply to the following territories forming part of the customs territory of the Community:

    (a) Mount Athos;

    (b) the Canary Islands;

    (c) the French territories referred to in Article 349 and Article 355(1) of the Treaty on the Functioning of the European Union;

    (d) the Åland Islands;

    (e) the Channel Islands.

2. This Directive shall not apply to the following territories not forming part of the customs territory of the Community:

    (a) the Island of Heligoland;

    (b) the territory of Büsingen;

    (c) Ceuta;

    (d) Melilla;

    (e) Livigno;

    (f) Campione d'Italia;

    (g) the Italian waters of Lake Lugano.

Article 7

1. In view of the conventions and treaties concluded with France, the United Kingdom and Cyprus respectively, the Principality of Monaco, the Isle of Man and the United Kingdom Sovereign Base Areas of Akrotiri and Dhekelia shall not be regarded, for the purposes of the application of this Directive, as third countries.

2. Member States shall take the measures necessary to ensure that transactions originating in or intended for the Principality of Monaco are treated as transactions originating in or intended for France, that transactions originating in or intended for the Isle of Man are treated as transactions originating in or intended for the United Kingdom, and that transactions originating in or intended for the United Kingdom Sovereign Base Areas of Akrotiri and Dhekelia are treated as transactions originating in or intended for Cyprus.

Article 8

If the Commission considers that the provisions laid down in Articles 6 and 7 are no longer justified, particularly in terms of fair competition or own resources, it shall present appropriate proposals to the Council.

Title III - Taxable Persons

Article 9

1. "Taxable person" shall mean any person who, independently, carries out in any place any economic activity, whatever the purpose or results of that activity.

Any activity of producers, traders or persons supplying services, including mining and agricultural activities and activities of the professions, shall be regarded as "economic activity". The exploitation of tangible or intangible property for the purposes of obtaining income therefrom on a continuing basis shall in particular be regarded as an economic activity.

2. In addition to the persons referred to in paragraph 1, any person who, on an occasional basis, supplies a new means of transport, which is dispatched or transported to the customer by the vendor or the customer, or on behalf of the vendor or the customer, to a destination outside the territory of a Member State but within the territory of the Community, shall be regarded as a taxable person.

Article 10

The condition in Article 9(1) that the economic activity be conducted "independently" shall exclude employed and other persons from VAT in so far as they are bound to an employer by a contract of employment or by any other legal ties creating the relationship of employer and employee as regards working conditions, remuneration and the employer's liability.

Article 11

After consulting the advisory committee on value added tax (hereafter, the "VAT Committee"), each Member State may regard as a single taxable person any persons established in the territory of that Member State who, while legally independent, are closely bound to one another by financial, economic and organizational links.

A Member State exercising the option provided for in the first paragraph, may adopt any measures needed to prevent tax evasion or avoidance through the use of this provision.

Article 12

1. Member States may regard as a taxable person anyone who carries out, on an occasional basis, a transaction relating to the activities referred to in the second subparagraph of Article 9(1) and in particular one of the following transactions:

    (a) the supply, before first occupation, of a building or parts of a building and of the land on which the building stands;

    (b) the supply of building land.

    For the purposes of paragraph 1(a), "building" shall mean any structure fixed to or in the ground.

2. Member States may lay down the detailed rules for applying the criterion referred to in paragraph 1 (a) to conversions of buildings and may determine what is meant by "the land on which a building stands".

    Member States may apply criteria other than that of first occupation, such as the period elapsing between the date of completion of the building and the date of first supply, or the period elapsing between the date of first occupation and the date of subsequent supply, provided that those periods do not exceed five years and two years respectively.

3. For the purposes of paragraph 1(b), "building land" shall mean any unimproved or improved land defined as such by the Member States.

Article 13

1. States, regional and local government authorities and other bodies governed by public law shall not be regarded as taxable persons in respect of the activities or transactions in which they engage as public authorities, even where they collect dues, fees, contributions or payments in connection with those activities or transactions.

    However, when they engage in such activities or transactions, they shall be regarded as taxable persons in respect of those activities or transactions where their treatment as non-taxable persons would lead to significant distortions of competition.

    In any event, bodies governed by public law shall be regarded as taxable persons in respect of the activities listed in Annex I, provided that those activities are not carried out on such a small scale as to be negligible.

RECAST VAT DIRECTIVE

2. Member States may regard activities, exempt under Articles 132, 135, 136 and 371, Articles 374 to 377, Article 378(2), Article 379(2) or Articles 380 to 390c, engaged in by bodies governed by public law as activities in which those bodies engage as public authorities.

Title IV - Taxable Transactions

Chapter 1 Supply of Goods

Article 14

1. "Supply of goods" shall mean the transfer of the right to dispose of tangible property as owner.

2. In addition to the transaction referred to in paragraph 1, each of the following shall be regarded as a supply of goods:

    (a) the transfer, by order made by or in the name of a public authority or in pursuance of the law, of the ownership of property against payment of compensation;

    (b) the actual handing over of goods pursuant to a contract for the hire of goods for a certain period, or for the sale of goods on deferred terms, which provides that in the normal course of events ownership is to pass at the latest upon payment of the final installment;

    (c) the transfer of goods pursuant to a contract under which commission is payable on purchase or sale.

3. Member States may regard the handing over of certain works of construction as a supply of goods.

Article 15

1. Electricity, gas, heat or cooling energy and the like shall be treated as tangible property.

2. Member States may regard the following as tangible property:

    (a) certain interests in immovable property;

    (b) rights in rem giving the holder thereof a right of use over immovable property;

    (c) shares or interests equivalent to shares giving the holder thereof de jure or de facto rights of ownership or possession over immovable property or part thereof.

Article 16

The application by a taxable person of goods forming part of his business assets for his private use or for that of his staff, or their disposal free of charge or, more generally, their application for purposes other than those of his business, shall be treated as a supply of goods for consideration, where the VAT on those goods or the component parts thereof was wholly or partly deductible.

However, the application of goods for business use as samples or as gifts of small value shall not be treated as a supply of goods for consideration.

RECAST VAT DIRECTIVE

Article 17

1. The transfer by a taxable person of goods forming part of his business assets to another Member State shall be treated as a supply of goods for consideration.

"Transfer to another Member State" shall mean the dispatch or transport of movable tangible property by or on behalf of the taxable person, for the purposes of his business, to a destination outside the territory of the Member State in which the property is located, but within the Community.

2. The dispatch or transport of goods for the purposes of any of the following transactions shall not be regarded as a transfer to another Member State:

    (a) the supply of the goods by the taxable person within the territory of the Member State in which the dispatch or transport ends, in accordance with the conditions laid down in Article 33;

    (b) the supply of the goods, for installation or assembly by or on behalf of the supplier, by the taxable person within the territory of the Member State in which dispatch or transport of the goods ends, in accordance with the conditions laid down in Article 36;

    (c) the supply of the goods by the taxable person on board a ship, an aircraft or a train in the course of a passenger transport operation, in accordance with the conditions laid down in Article 37;

    (d) the supply of gas through a natural gas system situated within the territory of the Community or any network connected to such a system, the supply of electricity or the supply of heat or cooling energy through heating or cooling networks, in accordance with the conditions laid down in Articles 38 and 39;

    (e) the supply of the goods by the taxable person within the territory of the Member State, in accordance with the conditions laid down in Articles 138, 146, 147, 148, 151 or 152;

    (f) the supply of a service performed for the taxable person and consisting in valuations of, or work on, the goods in question physically carried out within the territory of the Member State in which dispatch or transport of the goods ends, provided that the goods, after being valued or worked upon, are returned to that taxable person in the Member State from which they were initially dispatched or transported;

    (g) the temporary use of the goods within the territory of the Member State in which dispatch or transport of the goods ends, for the purposes of the supply of services by the taxable person established within the Member State in which dispatch or transport of the goods began;

    (h) the temporary use of the goods, for a period not exceeding twenty-four months, within the territory of another Member State, in which the importation of the same goods from a third country with a view to their temporary use would be covered by the arrangements for temporary importation with full exemption from import duties.

3. If one of the conditions governing eligibility under paragraph 2 is no longer met, the goods shall be regarded as having been transferred to another Member State. In such

cases, the transfer shall be deemed to take place at the time when that condition ceases to be met.

Article 18

Member States may treat each of the following transactions as a supply of goods for consideration:

- (a) the application by a taxable person for the purposes of his business of goods produced, constructed, extracted, processed, purchased or imported in the course of such business, where the VAT on such goods, had they been acquired from another taxable person, would not be wholly deductible;

- (b) the application of goods by a taxable person for the purposes of a non-taxable area of activity, where the VAT on such goods became wholly or partly deductible upon their acquisition or upon their application in accordance with point (a);

- (c) with the exception of the cases referred to in Article 19, the retention of goods by a taxable person, or by his successors, when he ceases to carry out a taxable economic activity, where the VAT on such goods became wholly or partly deductible upon their acquisition or upon their application in accordance with point (a).

Article 19

In the event of a transfer, whether for consideration or not or as a contribution to a company, of a totality of assets or part thereof, Member States may consider that no supply of goods has taken place and that the person to whom the goods are transferred is to be treated as the successor to the transferor.

Member States may, in cases where the recipient is not wholly liable to tax, take the measures necessary to prevent distortion of competition. They may also adopt any measures needed to prevent tax evasion or avoidance through the use of this Article.

Chapter 2 Intra-Community Acquisition of Goods

Article 20

"Intra-Community acquisition of goods" shall mean the acquisition of the right to dispose as owner of movable tangible property dispatched or transported to the person acquiring the goods, by or on behalf of the vendor or the person acquiring the goods, in a Member State other than that in which dispatch or transport of the goods began.

Where goods acquired by a non-taxable legal person are dispatched or transported from a third territory or a third country and imported by that non-taxable legal person into a Member State other than the Member State in which dispatch or transport of the goods ends, the goods shall be regarded as having been dispatched or transported from the Member State of importation. That Member State shall grant the importer designated or recognized under Article 201 as liable for payment of VAT a refund of the VAT paid in respect of the importation of the goods, provided that the importer establishes that VAT has been applied to his acquisition in the Member State in which dispatch or transport of the goods ends.

Article 21

The application by a taxable person, for the purposes of his business, of goods dispatched or transported by or on behalf of that taxable person from another Member State, within which the goods were produced, extracted, processed, purchased or acquired within the meaning of Article 2(1)(b), or into which they were imported by that taxable person for the purposes of his business, shall be treated as an intra-Community acquisition of goods for consideration.

Article 22

The application by the armed forces of a State party to the North Atlantic Treaty, for their use or for the use of the civilian staff accompanying them, of goods which they have not purchased subject to the general rules governing taxation on the domestic market of a Member State shall be treated as an intra-Community acquisition of goods for consideration, where the importation of those goods would not be eligible for the exemption provided for in Article 143(1)(h).

Article 23

Member States shall take the measures necessary to ensure that a transaction which would have been classed as a supply of goods if it had been carried out within their territory by a taxable person acting as such is classed as an intra-Community acquisition of goods.

Chapter 3 Supply of Services

Article 24

1. "Supply of services" shall mean any transaction which does not constitute a supply of goods.

2. "Telecommunications services" shall mean services relating to the transmission, emission or reception of signals, words, images and sounds or information of any nature by wire, radio, optical or other electromagnetic systems, including the related transfer or assignment of the right to use capacity for such transmission, emission or reception, with the inclusion of the provision of access to global information networks.

Article 25

A supply of services may consist, inter alia, in one of the following transactions:

- (a) the assignment of intangible property, whether or not the subject of a document establishing title;
- (b) the obligation to refrain from an act, or to tolerate an act or situation;
- (c) the performance of services in pursuance of an order made by or in the name of a public authority or in pursuance of the law.

Article 26

1. Each of the following transactions shall be treated as a supply of services for consideration:

    - (a) the use of goods forming part of the assets of a business for the private use of a taxable person or of his staff or, more generally, for purposes other than those of his business, where the VAT on such goods was wholly or partly deductible;
    - (b) the supply of services carried out free of charge by a taxable person for his private use or for that of his staff or, more generally, for purposes other than those of his business.

2. Member States may derogate from paragraph 1, provided that such derogation does not lead to distortion of competition.

Article 27

In order to prevent distortion of competition and after consulting the VAT Committee, Member States may treat as a supply of services for consideration the supply by a taxable person of a service for the purposes of his business, where the VAT on such a service, were it supplied by another taxable person, would not be wholly deductible.

Article 28

Where a taxable person acting in his own name but on behalf of another person takes part in a supply of services, he shall be deemed to have received and supplied those services himself.

Article 29

Article 19 shall apply in like manner to the supply of services.

Chapter 4 Importation of Goods

Article 30

"Importation of goods" shall mean the entry into the Community of goods which are not in free circulation within the meaning of Article 24 of the Treaty.

In addition to the transaction referred to in the first paragraph, the entry into the Community of goods which are in free circulation, coming from a third territory forming part of the customs territory of the Community, shall be regarded as importation of goods.

Title V - Place of Taxable Transactions

Chapter 1 Place of Supply of Goods

Section 1: Supply of Goods without Transport

Article 31

Where goods are not dispatched or transported, the place of supply shall be deemed to be the place where the goods are located at the time when the supply takes place.

Section 2: Supply of Goods with Transport

Article 32

Where goods are dispatched or transported by the supplier, or by the customer, or by a third person, the place of supply shall be deemed to be the place where the goods are located at the time when dispatch or transport of the goods to the customer begins.

However, if dispatch or transport of the goods begins in a third territory or third country, both the place of supply by the importer designated or recognized under Article 201 as liable for payment of VAT and the place of any subsequent supply shall be deemed to be within the Member State of importation of the goods.

Article 33

1. By way of derogation from Article 32, the place of supply of goods dispatched or transported by or on behalf of the supplier from a Member State other than that in which dispatch or transport of the goods ends shall be deemed to be the place where the goods are located at the time when dispatch or transport of the goods to the customer ends, where the following conditions are met:

    (a) the supply of goods is carried out for a taxable person, or a non-taxable legal person, whose intra-Community acquisitions of goods are not subject to VAT pursuant to Article 3(1) or for any other non-taxable person;

    (b) the goods supplied are neither new means of transport nor goods supplied after assembly or installation, with or without a trial run, by or on behalf of the supplier.

2. Where the goods supplied are dispatched or transported from a third territory or a third country and imported by the supplier into a Member State other than that in which dispatch or transport of the goods to the customer ends, they shall be regarded as having been dispatched or transported from the Member State of importation.

Article 34

1. Provided the following conditions are met, Article 33 shall not apply to supplies of goods all of which are dispatched or transported to the same Member State, where that Member State is the Member State in which dispatch or transport of the goods ends:

    (a) the goods supplied are not products subject to excise duty;

    (b) the total value, exclusive of VAT, of such supplies effected under the conditions laid down in Article 33 within that Member State does not in any one calendar year exceed EUR 100,000 or the equivalent in national currency;

    (d) the total value, exclusive of VAT, of the supplies of goods, other than products subject to excise duty, effected under the conditions laid down in Article 33 within that Member State did not in the previous calendar year exceed EUR 100,000 or the equivalent in national currency.

2. The Member State within the territory of which the goods are located at the time when their dispatch or transport to the customer ends may limit the threshold referred to in paragraph 1 to EUR 35,000 or the equivalent in national currency, where that Member State fears that the threshold of EUR 100,000 might cause serious distortion of competition.

Member States which exercise the option under the first subparagraph shall take the measures necessary to inform accordingly the competent public authorities in the Member State in which dispatch or transport of the goods begins.

3. The Commission shall present to the Council at the earliest opportunity a report on the operation of the special EUR 35,000 threshold referred to in paragraph 2, accompanied, if necessary, by appropriate proposals.

4. The Member State within the territory of which the goods are located at the time when their dispatch or transport begins shall grant those taxable persons who carry out supplies of goods eligible under paragraph 1 the right to opt for the place of supply to be determined in accordance with Article 33.

The Member States concerned shall lay down the detailed rules governing the exercise of the option referred to in the first subparagraph, which shall in any event cover two calendar years.

Article 35

Articles 33 and 34 shall not apply to supplies of second-hand goods, works of art, collectors' items or antiques, as defined in points (1) to (4) of Article 311(1), nor to supplies of second-hand means of transport, as defined in Article 327(3), subject to VAT in accordance with the relevant special arrangements.

Article 36

Where goods dispatched or transported by the supplier, by the customer or by a third person are installed or assembled, with or without a trial run, by or on behalf of the supplier, the place of supply shall be deemed to be the place where the goods are installed or assembled.

Where the installation or assembly is carried out in a Member State other than that of the supplier, the Member State within the territory of which the installation or assembly is carried out shall take the measures necessary to ensure that there is no double taxation in that Member State.

Section 3: Supply of goods on board ships, aircraft or trains

Article 37

1. Where goods are supplied on board ships, aircraft or trains during the section of a passenger transport operation effected within the Community, the place of supply shall be deemed to be at the point of departure of the passenger transport operation.
2. For the purposes of paragraph 1, "section of a passenger transport operation effected within the Community" shall mean the section of the operation effected, without a stopover outside the Community, between the point of departure and the point of arrival of the passenger transport operation.

"Point of departure of a passenger transport operation" shall mean the first scheduled point of passenger embarkation within the Community, where applicable after a stopover outside the Community.

"Point of arrival of a passenger transport operation" shall mean the last scheduled point of disembarkation within the Community of passengers who embarked in the Community, where applicable before a stopover outside the Community.

In the case of a return trip, the return leg shall be regarded as a separate transport operation.

3. The Commission shall, at the earliest opportunity, present to the Council a report, accompanied if necessary by appropriate proposals, on the place of taxation of the supply of goods for consumption on board and the supply of services, including restaurant services, for passengers on board ships, aircraft or trains.

Pending adoption of the proposals referred to in the first subparagraph, Member States may exempt or continue to exempt, with deductibility of the VAT paid at the preceding stage, the supply of goods for consumption on board in respect of which the place of taxation is determined in accordance with paragraph 1.

RECAST VAT DIRECTIVE

Section 4: Supplies of gas through a natural gas system, of electricity and of heat or cooling energy through heating and cooling networks

Article 38

In the case of the supply of gas through a natural gas system situated within the territory of the Community or any network connected to such a system, the supply of electricity, or the supply of heat or cooling energy through heating or cooling networks to a taxable dealer, the place of supply shall be deemed to be the place where that taxable dealer has established his business or has a fixed establishment for which the goods are supplied or, in the absence of such a place of business or fixed establishment, the place where he has his permanent address or usually resides..

For the purposes of paragraph 1, "taxable dealer" shall mean a taxable person whose principal activity in respect of purchases of gas, electricity, heat or cooling energy is reselling those products and whose own consumption of those products is negligible.

Article 39

In the case of the supply of gas through a natural gas system situated within the territory of the Community or any network connected to such a system, the supply of electricity or the supply of heat or cooling energy through heating or cooling networks, where such a supply is not covered by Article 38, the place of supply shall be deemed to be the place where the customer effectively uses and consumes the goods..

Where all or part of the gas, electricity or heat or cooling energy is not effectively consumed by the customer, those non-consumed goods shall be deemed to have been used and consumed at the place where the customer has established his business or has a fixed establishment for which the goods are supplied. In the absence of such a place of business or fixed establishment, the customer shall be deemed to have used and consumed the goods at the place where he has his permanent address or usually resides.

Chapter 2 Place of an Intra-Community Acquisition of Goods

Article 40

The place of an intra-Community acquisition of goods shall be deemed to be the place where dispatch or transport of the goods to the person acquiring them ends.

Article 41

Without prejudice to Article 40, the place of an intra-Community acquisition of goods as referred to in Article 2(1)(b)(i) shall be deemed to be within the territory of the Member State which issued the VAT identification number under which the person acquiring the goods made the acquisition, unless the person acquiring the goods establishes that VAT has been applied to that acquisition in accordance with Article 40.

If VAT is applied to the acquisition in accordance with the first paragraph and subsequently applied, pursuant to Article 40, to the acquisition in the Member State in which dispatch or transport of the goods ends, the taxable amount shall be reduced accordingly in the Member State which issued the VAT identification number under which the person acquiring the goods made the acquisition.

Article 42

The first paragraph of Article 41 shall not apply and VAT shall be deemed to have been applied to the intra-Community acquisition of goods in accordance with Article 40 where the following conditions are met:

(a) the person acquiring the goods establishes that he has made the intra-Community acquisition for the purposes of a subsequent supply, within the territory of the Member State identified in accordance with Article 40, for which the person to whom the supply is made has been designated in accordance with Article 197 as liable for payment of VAT;

(b) the person acquiring the goods has satisfied the obligations laid down in Article 265 relating to submission of the recapitulative statement.

RECAST VAT DIRECTIVE

Chapter 3 Place of Supply of Services

Section 1: Definitions

Article 43

For the purpose of applying the rules concerning the place of supply of services:

1. a taxable person who also carries out activities or transactions that are not considered to be taxable supplies of goods or services in accordance with Article 2(1) shall be regarded as a taxable person in respect of all services rendered to him;

2. a non-taxable legal person who is identified for VAT purposes shall be regarded as a taxable person.

Section 2: General rules

Article 44

The place of supply of services to a taxable person acting as such shall be the place where that person has established his business. However, if those services are provided to a fixed establishment of the taxable person located in a place other than the place where he has established his business, the place of supply of those services shall be the place where that fixed establishment is located. In the absence of such place of establishment or fixed establishment, the place of supply of services shall be the place where the taxable person who receives such services has his permanent address or usually resides.

Article 45

The place of supply of services to a non-taxable person shall be the place where the supplier has established his business. However, if those services are provided from a fixed establishment of the supplier located in a place other than the place where he has established his business, the place of supply of those services shall be the place where that fixed establishment is located. In the absence of such place of establishment or fixed establishment, the place of supply of services shall be the place where the supplier has his permanent address or usually resides.

Section 3: Particular provisions

Subsection 1: Supply of services by intermediaries

Article 46

The place of supply of services rendered to a non-taxable person by an intermediary acting in the name and on behalf of another person shall be the place where the underlying transaction is supplied in accordance with this Directive.

Subsection 2: Supply of services connected with immovable property

Article 47

The place of supply of services connected with immovable property, including the services of experts and estate agents, the provision of accommodation in the hotel sector or in sectors with a similar function, such as holiday camps or sites developed for use as camping sites, the granting of rights to use immovable property and services for the preparation and coordination of construction work, such as the services of architects and of firms providing on-site supervision, shall be the place where the immovable property is located.

Subsection 3: Supply of transport

Article 48

The place of supply of passenger transport shall be the place where the transport takes place, proportionate to the distances covered.

Article 49

The place of supply of the transport of goods, other than the intra-Community transport of goods, to non-taxable persons shall be the place where the transport takes place, proportionate to the distances covered.

Article 50

The place of supply of the intra-Community transport of goods to non-taxable persons shall be the place of departure.

Article 51

"Intra-Community transport of goods" shall mean any transport of goods in respect of which the place of departure and the place of arrival are situated within the territories of two different Member States.

Place of departure" shall mean the place where transport of the goods actually begins, irrespective of distances covered in order to reach the place where the goods are located and "place of arrival" shall mean the place where transport of the goods actually ends.

Article 52

Member States need not apply VAT to that part of the intra-Community transport of goods to non-taxable persons taking place over waters which do not form part of the territory of the Community.

Subsection 4: Supply of cultural, artistic, sporting, scientific, educational, entertainment and similar services, ancillary transport services and valuations of and work on movable property

Article 53

The place of supply of services in respect of admission to cultural, artistic, sporting, scientific, educational, entertainment or similar events, such as fairs and exhibitions, and of ancillary services related to the admission, supplied to a taxable person, shall be the place where those events actually take place.

Article 54

1. The place of supply of services and ancillary services, relating to cultural, artistic, sporting, scientific, educational, entertainment or similar activities, such as fairs and exhibitions, including the supply of services of the organizers of such activities, supplied to a non-taxable person shall be the place where those activities actually take place.

2. The place of supply of the following services to a non-taxable person shall be the place where the services are physically carried out:

    (a) ancillary transport activities such as loading, unloading, handling and similar activities

    (b) valuations of and work on movable tangible property.

Subsection 5: Supply of restaurant and catering services

Article 55

The place of supply of restaurant and catering services other than those physically carried out on board ships, aircraft or trains during the section of a passenger transport operation effected within the Community, shall be the place where the services are physically carried out.

Subsection 6: Hiring of means of transport

Article 56

1. The place of short-term hiring of a means of transport shall be the place where the means of transport is actually put at the disposal of the customer.

2. The place of hiring, other than short-term hiring, of a means of transport to a non-taxable person shall be the place where the customer is established, has his permanent address or usually resides.

3. However, the place of hiring a pleasure boat to a non-taxable person, other than short-term hiring, shall be the place where the pleasure boat is actually put at the disposal of the customer, where this service is actually provided by the supplier from his place of business or a fixed establishment situated in that place.

4. For the purposes of paragraphs 1 and 2, "short-term" shall mean the continuous possession or use of the means of transport throughout a period of not more than thirty days and, in the case of vessels, not more than 90 days.

Subsection 7: Supply of restaurant and catering services for consumption on board ships, aircraft or trains

Article 57

1. The place of supply of restaurant and catering services which are physically carried out on board ships, aircraft or trains during the section of a passenger transport operation effected within the Community, shall be at the point of departure of the passenger transport operation.

2. For the purposes of paragraph 1, "section of a passenger transport operation effected within the Community" shall mean the section of the operation effected, without a stopover outside the Community, between the point of departure and the point of arrival of the passenger transport operation.

"Point of departure of a passenger transport operation" shall mean the first scheduled point of passenger embarkation within the Community, where applicable after a stopover outside the Community.

"Point of arrival of a passenger transport operation" shall mean the last scheduled point of disembarkation within the Community of passengers who embarked in the Community, where applicable before a stopover outside the Community.

In the case of a return trip, the return leg shall be regarded as a separate transport operation.

Subsection 8: Supply of electronic services to non-taxable persons

Article 58

The place of supply of electronically supplied services, in particular those referred to in Annex II, when supplied to non-taxable persons who are established in a Member State, or who have their permanent address or usually reside in a Member State, by a taxable person who has established his business outside the Community or has a fixed establishment there from which the service is supplied, or who, in the absence of such a place of business or fixed establishment, has his permanent address or usually resides outside the Community, shall be the place where the non-taxable person is established, or where he has his permanent address or usually resides.

Where the supplier of a service and the customer communicate via electronic mail, that shall not of itself mean that the service supplied is an electronically supplied service.

Subsection 9: Supply of services to non-taxable persons outside the Community

Article 59

The place of supply of the following services to a non-taxable person who is established or has his permanent address or usually resides outside the Community, shall be the place where that person is established, has his permanent address or usually resides:

(a) transfers and assignments of copyrights, patents, licenses, trade marks and similar rights;

(b) advertising services;

(c) the services of consultants, engineers, consultancy firms, lawyers, accountants and other similar services, as well as data processing and the provision of information;

(d) obligations to refrain from pursuing or exercising, in whole or in part, a business activity or a right referred to in this Article;

(e) banking, financial and insurance transactions including reinsurance, with the exception of the hire of safes;

(f) the supply of staff;

(g) the hiring out of movable tangible property, with the exception of all means of transport;

(h) the provision of access to a natural gas system situated within the territory of the Community or to any network connected to such a system, to the electricity system or to heating or cooling networks, or the transmission or distribution through these systems or networks, and the provision of other services directly linked thereto;

(i) telecommunications services;

(j)   radio and television broadcasting services;

(k)   electronically supplied services, in particular those referred to in Annex II.

Where the supplier of a service and the customer communicate via electronic mail, that shall not of itself mean that the service supplied is an electronically supplied service.

Subsection 10: Prevention of double taxation or non-taxation

Article 59a

In order to prevent double taxation, non-taxation or distortion of competition, Member States may, with regard to services the place of supply of which is governed by Articles 44, 45, 56 and 59:

(a)   consider the place of supply of any or all of those services, if situated within their territory, as being situated outside the Community if the effective use and enjoyment of the services takes place outside the Community;

(b)   consider the place of supply of any or all of those services, if situated outside the Community, as being situated within their territory if the effective use and enjoyment of the services takes place within their territory.

However, this provision shall not apply to the electronically supplied services where those services are rendered to non-taxable persons not established within the Community.

Article 59b

Member States shall apply Article 59a(b) to telecommunications services and radio and television broadcasting services, as referred to in point (j) of the first paragraph of Article 59, supplied to non-taxable persons who are established in a Member State, or who have their permanent address or usually reside in a Member State, by a taxable person who has established his business outside the Community or has a fixed establishment there from which the services are supplied, or who, in the absence of such a place of business or fixed establishment, has his permanent address or usually resides outside the Community.

Chapter 4 Place of Importation of Goods

Article 60

The place of importation of goods shall be the Member State within whose territory the goods are located when they enter the Community.

Article 61

By way of derogation from Article 60, where, on entry into the Community, goods which are not in free circulation are placed under one of the arrangements or situations referred to in Article 156, or under temporary importation arrangements with total exemption from import duty, or under external transit arrangements, the place of importation of such goods shall be the Member State within whose territory the goods cease to be covered by those arrangements or situations.

Similarly, where, on entry into the Community, goods which are in free circulation are placed under one of the arrangements or situations referred to in Articles 276 and 277, the place of importation shall be the Member State within whose territory the goods cease to be covered by those arrangements or situations.

Title VI - Chargeable Event and chargeability of VAT

Chapter 1 General Provisions

Article 62

For the purposes of this Directive:

(1) "chargeable event" shall mean the occurrence by virtue of which the legal conditions necessary for VAT to become chargeable are fulfilled;

(2) VAT shall become "chargeable" when the tax authority becomes entitled under the law, at a given moment, to claim the tax from the person liable to pay, even though the time of payment may be deferred.

Chapter 2 Supply of Goods or Services

Article 63

The chargeable event shall occur and VAT shall become chargeable when the goods or the services are supplied.

Article 64

1. Where it gives rise to successive statements of account or successive payments, the supply of goods, other than that consisting in the hire of goods for a certain period or the sale of goods on deferred terms, as referred to in point (b) of Article 14(2), or the supply of services shall be regarded as being completed on expiry of the periods to which such statements of account or payments relate.

2. Continuous supplies of goods over a period of more than one calendar month which are dispatched or transported to a Member State other than that in which the dispatch or transport of those goods begins and which are supplied VAT-exempt or which are transferred VAT-exempt to another Member State by a taxable person for the purposes of his business, in accordance with the conditions laid down in Article 138, shall be regarded as being completed on expiry of each calendar month until such time as the supply comes to an end.

Supplies of services for which VAT is payable by the customer pursuant to Article 196, which are supplied continuously over a period of more than one year and which do not give rise to statements of account or payments during that period, shall be regarded as being completed on expiry of each calendar year until such time as the supply of services comes to an end.

Member States may provide that, in certain cases other than those referred to in the first and second subparagraphs, the continuous supply of goods or services over a period of time is to be regarded as being completed at least at intervals of one year.

Article 65

Where a payment is to be made on account before the goods or services are supplied, VAT shall become chargeable on receipt of the payment and on the amount received.

Article 66

By way of derogation from Articles 63, 64 and 65, Member States may provide that VAT is to become chargeable, in respect of certain transactions or certain categories of taxable person at one of the following times:

(a) no later than the time the invoice is issued;

(b) no later than the time the payment is received;

(c) where an invoice is not issued, or is issued late, within a specified time no later than on expiry of the time-limit for issue of invoices imposed by Member States pursuant to the second paragraph of Article 222 or where no such time-limit has been imposed by the Member State, within a specified period from the date of the chargeable event.

The derogation provided for in the first paragraph shall not, however, apply to supplies of services in respect of which VAT is payable by the customer pursuant to Article 196 and to supplies or transfers of goods referred to in Article 67.

Article 67

Where, in accordance with the conditions laid down in Article 138, goods dispatched or transported to a Member State other than that in which dispatch or transport of the goods begins are supplied VAT-exempt or where goods are transferred VAT-exempt to another Member State by a taxable person for the purposes of his business, VAT shall become chargeable on issue of the invoice, or on expiry of the time limit referred to in the first paragraph of Article 222 if no invoice has been issued by that time.

Article 64(1), the third subparagraph of Article 64(2) and Article 65 shall not apply with respect to the supplies and transfers of goods referred to in the first paragraph.

Chapter 3 Intra-Community Acquisition of Goods

Article 68

The chargeable event shall occur when the intra-Community acquisition of goods is made.

The intra-Community acquisition of goods shall be regarded as being made when the supply of similar goods is regarded as being effected within the territory of the relevant Member State.

Article 69

In the case of the intra-Community acquisition of goods, VAT shall become chargeable on issue of the invoice, or on expiry of the time limit referred to in the first paragraph of Article 222 if no invoice has been issued by that time.

Chapter 4 Importation of Goods

Article 70

The chargeable event shall occur and VAT shall become chargeable when the goods are imported.

Article 71

1. Where, on entry into the Community, goods are placed under one of the arrangements or situations referred to in Articles 156, 276 and 277, or under temporary importation arrangements with total exemption from import duty, or under external transit arrangements, the chargeable event shall occur and VAT shall become chargeable only when the goods cease to be covered by those arrangements or situations.

However, where imported goods are subject to customs duties, to agricultural levies or to charges having equivalent effect established under a common policy, the chargeable event shall occur and VAT shall become chargeable when the chargeable event in respect of those duties occurs and those duties become chargeable.

2. Where imported goods are not subject to any of the duties referred to in the second subparagraph of paragraph 1, Member States shall, as regards the chargeable event and the moment when VAT becomes chargeable, apply the provisions in force governing customs duties.

Title VII - Taxable Amount

Chapter 1 Definition

Article 72

For the purposes of this Directive, "open market value" shall mean the full amount that, in order to obtain the goods or services in question at that time, a customer at the same marketing stage at which the supply of goods or services takes place, would have to pay, under conditions of fair competition, to a supplier at arm's length within the territory of the Member State in which the supply is subject to tax.

Where no comparable supply of goods or services can be ascertained, "open market value" shall mean the following:

(1) in respect of goods, an amount that is not less than the purchase price of the goods or of similar goods or, in the absence of a purchase price, the cost price, determined at the time of supply;

(2) in respect of services, an amount that is not less than the full cost to the taxable person of providing the service.

Chapter 2 Supply of Goods or Services

Article 73

In respect of the supply of goods or services, other than as referred to in Articles 74 to 77, the taxable amount shall include everything which constitutes consideration obtained or to be obtained by the supplier, in return for the supply, from the customer or a third party, including subsidies directly linked to the price of the supply.

Article 74

Where a taxable person applies or disposes of goods forming part of his business assets, or where goods are retained by a taxable person, or by his successors, when his taxable economic activity ceases, as referred to in Articles 16 and 18, the taxable amount shall be the purchase price of the goods or of similar goods or, in the absence of a purchase price, the cost price, determined at the time when the application, disposal or retention takes place.

Article 75

In respect of the supply of services, as referred to in Article 26, where goods forming part of the assets of a business are used for private purposes or services are carried out free of charge, the taxable amount shall be the full cost to the taxable person of providing the services.

Article 76

In respect of the supply of goods consisting in transfer to another Member State, the taxable amount shall be the purchase price of the goods or of similar goods or, in the absence of a purchase price, the cost price, determined at the time the transfer takes place.

Article 77

In respect of the supply by a taxable person of a service for the purposes of his business, as referred to in Article 27, the taxable amount shall be the open market value of the service supplied.

Article 78

The taxable amount shall include the following factors:

    (a)   taxes, duties, levies and charges, excluding the VAT itself;

(b) incidental expenses, such as commission, packing, transport and insurance costs, charged by the supplier to the customer.

For the purposes of point (b) of the first paragraph, Member States may regard expenses covered by a separate agreement as incidental expenses.

Article 79

The taxable amount shall not include the following factors:

(a) price reductions by way of discount for early payment;

(b) price discounts and rebates granted to the customer and obtained by him at the time of the supply;

(c) amounts received by a taxable person from the customer, as repayment of expenditure incurred in the name and on behalf of the customer, and entered in his books in a suspense account.

The taxable person must furnish proof of the actual amount of the expenditure referred to in point (c) of the first paragraph and may not deduct any VAT which may have been charged.

Article 80

1. In order to prevent tax evasion or avoidance, Member States may in any of the following cases take measures to ensure that, in respect of the supply of goods or services involving family or other close personal ties, management, ownership, membership, financial or legal ties as defined by the Member State, the taxable amount is to be the open market value:

    (a) where the consideration is lower than the open market value and the recipient of the supply does not have a full right of deduction under Articles 167 to 171 and Articles 173 to 177;

    (b) where the consideration is lower than the open market value and the supplier does not have a full right of deduction under Articles 167 to 171 and Articles 173 to 177 and the supply is subject to an exemption under Articles 132, 135, 136, 371, 375, 376, 377, 378(2), 379(2) or Articles 380 to 390c;

    (c) where the consideration is higher than the open market value and the supplier does not have a full right of deduction under Articles 167 to 171 and Articles 173 to 177.

For the purposes of the first subparagraph, legal ties may include the relationship between an employer and employee or the employee's family, or any other closely connected persons.

2. Where Member States exercise the option provided for in paragraph 1, they may restrict the categories of suppliers or recipients to whom the measures shall apply.

3. Member States shall inform the VAT Committee of national legislative measures adopted pursuant to paragraph 1 in so far as these are not measures authorized by

the Council prior to 13 August 2006 in accordance with Article 27 (1) to (4) of Directive 77/388/EEC, and which are continued under paragraph 1 of this Article.

Article 81

Member States which, at 1 January 1993, were not availing themselves of the option under Article 98 of applying a reduced rate may, if they avail themselves of the option under Article 89, provide that in respect of the supply of works of art, as referred to in Article 103(2), the taxable amount is to be equal to a fraction of the amount determined in accordance with Articles 73, 74, 76, 78 and 79.

The fraction referred to in the first paragraph shall be determined in such a way that the VAT thus due is equal to at least 5 % of the amount determined in accordance with Articles 73, 74, 76, 78 and 79.

Article 82

Member States may provide that, in respect of the supply of goods and services, the taxable amount is to include the value of exempt investment gold within the meaning of Article 346, which has been provided by the customer to be used as basis for working and which as a result, loses its VAT exempt investment gold status when such goods and services are supplied. The value to be used is the open market value of the investment gold at the time that those goods and services are supplied.

Chapter 3 Intra-Community Acquisition of Goods

Article 83

In respect of the intra-Community acquisition of goods, the taxable amount shall be established on the basis of the same factors as are used in accordance with Chapter 1 to determine the taxable amount for the supply of the same goods within the territory of the Member State concerned. In the case of the transactions, to be treated as intra-Community acquisitions of goods, referred to in Articles 21 and 22, the taxable amount shall be the purchase price of the goods or of similar goods or, in the absence of a purchase price, the cost price, determined at the time of the supply.

Article 84

1. Member States shall take the measures necessary to ensure that the excise duty due from or paid by the person making the intra-Community acquisition of a product subject to excise duty is included in the taxable amount in accordance with point (a) of the first paragraph of Article 78.

2. Where, after the intra-Community acquisition of goods has been made, the person acquiring the goods obtains a refund of the excise duty paid in the Member State in which dispatch or transport of the goods began, the taxable amount shall be reduced accordingly in the Member State in the territory of which the acquisition was made.

Chapter 4 Importation of Goods

Article 85

In respect of the importation of goods, the taxable amount shall be the value for customs purposes, determined in accordance with the Community provisions in force.

Article 86

1. The taxable amount shall include the following factors, in so far as they are not already included:

    (a) taxes, duties, levies and other charges due outside the Member State of importation, and those due by reason of importation, excluding the VAT to be levied;

    (b) incidental expenses, such as commission, packing, transport and insurance costs, incurred up to the first place of destination within the territory of the Member State of importation as well as those resulting from transport to another place of destination within the Community, if that other place is known when the chargeable event occurs.

2. For the purposes of point (b) of paragraph 1, "first place of destination" shall mean the place mentioned on the consignment note or on any other document under which the goods are imported into the Member State of importation. If no such mention is made, the first place of destination shall be deemed to be the place of the first transfer of cargo in the Member State of importation.

Article 87

The taxable amount shall not include the following factors:

(a) price reductions by way of discount for early payment;

(b) price discounts and rebates granted to the customer and obtained by him at the time of importation.

Article 88

Where goods temporarily exported from the Community are re-imported after having undergone, outside the Community, repair, processing, adaptation, making up or re-working, Member States shall take steps to ensure that the tax treatment of the goods for VAT purposes is the same as that which would have been applied had the repair, processing, adaptation, making up or re-working been carried out within their territory.

Article 89

Member States which, at 1 January 1993, were not availing themselves of the option under Article 98 of applying a reduced rate may provide that in respect of the importation of works of art, collectors' items and antiques, as defined in points (2), (3) and (4) of Article 311(1), the taxable amount is to be equal to a fraction of the amount determined in accordance with Articles 85, 86 and 87.

The fraction referred to in the first paragraph shall be determined in such a way that the VAT thus due on the importation is equal to at least 5 % of the amount determined in accordance with Articles 85, 86 and 87.

Chapter 5 Miscellaneous Provisions

Article 90

1. In the case of cancellation, refusal or total or partial non-payment, or where the price is reduced after the supply takes place, the taxable amount shall be reduced accordingly under conditions which shall be determined by the Member States.

2. In the case of total or partial non-payment, Member States may derogate from paragraph 1.

Article 91

1. Where the factors used to determine the taxable amount on importation are expressed in a currency other than that of the Member State in which assessment takes place, the exchange rate shall be determined in accordance with the Community provisions governing the calculation of the value for customs purposes.

2. Member States shall accept instead the use of the latest exchange rate published by the European Central Bank at the time the tax becomes chargeable. Conversion between currencies other than the euro shall be made by using the euro exchange rate of each currency. Member States may require that they be notified of the exercise of this option by the taxable person.

However, for some of the transactions referred to in the first subparagraph or for certain categories of taxable persons, Member States may use the exchange rate determined in accordance with the Community provisions in force governing the calculation of the value for customs purposes.

Article 92

As regards the costs of returnable packing material, Member States may take one of the following measures:

(a) exclude them from the taxable amount and take the measures necessary to ensure that this amount is adjusted if the packing material is not returned;

(b) include them in the taxable amount and take the measures necessary to ensure that this amount is adjusted if the packing material is in fact returned.

Title VIII - Rates

Chapter 1 Application of Rates

Article 93

The rate applicable to taxable transactions shall be that in force at the time of the chargeable event.

However, in the following situations, the rate applicable shall be that in force when VAT becomes chargeable:

(a) in the cases referred to in Articles 65 and 66;

(b) in the case of an intra-Community acquisition of goods;

(c) in the cases, concerning the importation of goods, referred to in the second subparagraph of Article 71(1) and in Article 71(2).

Article 94

1. The rate applicable to the intra-Community acquisition of goods shall be that applied to the supply of like goods within the territory of the Member State.

2. Subject to the option under Article 103(1) of applying a reduced rate to the importation of works of art, collectors' items or antiques, the rate applicable to the importation of goods shall be that applied to the supply of like goods within the territory of the Member State.

Article 95

Where rates are changed, Member States may, in the cases referred to in Articles 65 and 66, effect adjustments in order to take account of the rate applying at the time when the goods or services were supplied.

Member States may also adopt all appropriate transitional measures.

Chapter 2 Structure and level of Rates

Section 1: Standard Rate

Article 96

Member States shall apply a standard rate of VAT, which shall be fixed by each Member State as a percentage of the taxable amount and which shall be the same for the supply of goods and for the supply of services.

Article 97

From 1 January 2011 until 31 December 2015, the standard rate may not be lower than 15 %

Section 2: Reduced Rates

Article 98

1. Member States may apply either one or two reduced rates.

2. The reduced rates shall apply only to supplies of goods or services in the categories set out in Annex III.

The reduced rates shall not apply to electronically supplied services.

3. When applying the reduced rates provided for in paragraph 1 to categories of goods, Member States may use the Combined Nomenclature to establish the precise coverage of the category concerned.

Article 99

1. The reduced rates shall be fixed as a percentage of the taxable amount, which may not be less than 5 %.

2. Each reduced rate shall be so fixed that the amount of VAT resulting from its application is such that the VAT deductible under Articles 167 to 171 and Articles 173 to 177 can normally be deducted in full.

Article 100

On the basis of a report from the Commission, the Council shall, starting in 1994, review the scope of the reduced rates every two years.

The Council may, in accordance with Article 93 of the Treaty, decide to alter the list of goods and services set out in Annex III.

Article 101

By 30 June 2007 at the latest the Commission shall present to the European Parliament and the Council an overall assessment report on the impact of reduced rates applying to locally supplied services, including restaurant services, notably in terms of job creation, economic growth and the proper functioning of the internal market, based on a study carried out by an independent economic think-tank.

Section 3: Particular Provisions

Article 102

After consultation of the VAT Committee, each Member State may apply a reduced rate to the supply of natural gas, electricity or district heating.

Article 103

1. Member States may provide that the reduced rate, or one of the reduced rates, which they apply in accordance with Articles 98 and 99 is also to apply to the importation of works of art, collectors' items and antiques, as defined in points (2), (3) and (4) of Article 311(1).

2. If Member States avail themselves of the option under paragraph 1, they may also apply the reduced rate to the following transactions:

    (a) the supply of works of art, by their creator or his successors in title;

    (b) the supply of works of art, on an occasional basis, by a taxable person other than a taxable dealer, where the works of art have been imported by the taxable person himself, or where they have been supplied to him by their creator or his successors in title, or where they have entitled him to full deduction of VAT.

Article 104

Austria may, in the communes of Jungholz and Mittelberg (Kleines Walsertal), apply a second standard rate which is lower than the corresponding rate applied in the rest of Austria but not less than 15 %.

Article 104a

Cyprus may apply one of the two reduced rates provided for in Article 98 to the supply of liquid petroleum gas (LPG) in cylinders.

Article 105

1. Portugal may apply one of the two reduced rates provided for in Article 98 to the tolls on bridges in the Lisbon area.

2. Portugal may, in the case of transactions carried out in the autonomous regions of the Azores and Madeira and of direct importation into those regions, apply rates lower than those applying on the mainland.

Chapter 3

Article 106-108 [Deleted].

Chapter 4 Special Provisions applying until the Adoption of Definitive Arrangements

Article 109

Pending introduction of the definitive arrangements referred to in Article 402, the provisions laid down in this Chapter shall apply.

Article 110

Member States which, at 1 January 1991, were granting exemptions with deductibility of the VAT paid at the preceding stage or applying reduced rates lower than the minimum laid down in Article 99 may continue to grant those exemptions or apply those reduced rates.

The exemptions and reduced rates referred to in the first paragraph must be in accordance with Community law and must have been adopted for clearly defined social reasons and for the benefit of the final consumer.

Article 111

Subject to the conditions laid down in the second paragraph of Article 110, exemptions with deductibility of the VAT paid at the preceding stage may continue to be granted in the following cases:

(a) by Finland in respect of the supply of newspapers and periodicals sold by subscription and the printing of publications distributed to the members of corporations for the public good;

(b) by Sweden in respect of the supply of newspapers, including radio and cassette newspapers for the visually impaired, pharmaceutical products supplied to hospitals or on prescription, and the production of, or other related services concerning, periodicals of non-profit-making organizations.

(c) by Malta in respect of the supply of foodstuffs for human consumption and pharmaceuticals.

Article 112

If the provisions of Article 110 cause for Ireland distortion of competition in the supply of energy products for heating and lighting, Ireland may, on specific request, be authorized by the Commission to apply a reduced rate to such supplies, in accordance with Articles 98 and 99.

In the case referred to in the first paragraph, Ireland shall submit a request to the Commission, together with all necessary information. If the Commission has not taken a decision within three months of receiving the request, Ireland shall be deemed to be authorized to apply the reduced rates proposed.

Article 113

Member States which, at 1 January 1991, in accordance with Community law, were granting exemptions with deductibility of the VAT paid at the preceding stage or applying reduced rates lower than the minimum laid down in Article 99, in respect of goods and services other than those specified in Annex III, may apply the reduced rate, or one of the two reduced rates, provided for in Article 98 to the supply of such goods or services.

Article 114

1. Member States which, on 1 January 1993, were obliged to increase their standard rate in force at 1 January 1991 by more than 2 % may apply a reduced rate lower than the minimum laid down in Article 99 to the supply of goods and services in the categories set out in Annex III.

The Member States referred to in the first subparagraph may also apply such a rate to children's clothing and children's footwear and housing.

2. Member States may not rely on paragraph 1 to introduce exemptions with deductibility of the VAT paid at the preceding stage.

Article 115

Member States which, at 1 January 1991, were applying a reduced rate to children's clothing children's footwear or housing may continue to apply such a rate to the supply of those goods or services.

Article 116

[Deleted]

Article 117

1. [Deleted].

2. Austria may apply one of the two reduced rates provided for in Article 98 to the letting of immovable property for residential use, provided that the rate is not lower than 10 %.

Article 118

Member States which, at 1 January 1991, were applying a reduced rate to the supply of goods or services other than those specified in Annex III may apply the reduced rate, or one of the two reduced rates, provided for in Article 98 to the supply of those goods or services, provided that the rate is not lower than 12 %.

The first paragraph shall not apply to the supply of second-hand goods, works of art, collectors' items or antiques, as defined in points (1) to (4) of Article 311(1), subject to VAT in accordance with the margin scheme provided for in Articles 312 to 325 or the arrangements for sales by public auction.

Article 119

For the purposes of applying Article 118, Austria may apply a reduced rate to wines produced on an agricultural holding by the producer-farmer, provided that the rate is not lower than 12 %.

Article 120

Greece may apply rates up to 30 % lower than the corresponding rates applied in mainland Greece in the departments of Lesbos, Chios, Samos, the Dodecanese and the Cyclades, and on the islands of Thassos, the Northern Sporades, Samothrace and Skiros.

Article 121

Member States which, at 1 January 1993, regarded work under contract as the supply of goods may apply to the delivery of work under contract the rate applicable to the goods obtained after execution of the work under contract.

For the purposes of applying the first paragraph, "delivery of work under contract" shall mean the handing over by a contractor to his customer of movable property made or assembled by the contractor from materials or objects entrusted to him by the customer for that purpose, whether or not the contractor has provided any part of the materials used.

Article 122

Member States may apply a reduced rate to the supply of live plants and other floricultural products, including bulbs, roots and the like, cut flowers and ornamental foliage, and of wood for use as firewood.

RECAST VAT DIRECTIVE

Chapter 5 Temporary Provisions

Article 123

The Czech Republic may, until 31 December 2010, continue to apply a reduced rate of not less than 5 % to the supply of construction work for residential housing not provided as part of a social policy, excluding building materials.

Article 124

[Deleted]

Article 125

1. Cyprus may, until 31 December 2010, continue to grant an exemption with deductibility of VAT paid at the preceding stage in respect of the supply of pharmaceuticals and foodstuffs for human consumption, with the exception of ice cream, ice lollies, frozen yoghurt, water ice and similar products and savory food products (potato crisps/sticks, puffs and similar products packaged for human consumption without further preparation).

2. [Deleted].

Article 126

[Deleted]

Article 127

[Deleted]

Article 128

1. Poland may, until 31 December 2010, grant an exemption with deductibility of VAT paid at the preceding stage in respect of the supply of certain books and specialist periodicals.

2. [Deleted].

3. Poland may, until 31 December 2010, continue to apply a reduced rate of not less than 3 % to the supply of foodstuffs as referred to in point (1) of Annex III.

4. Poland may, until 31 December 2010, continue to apply a reduced rate of not less than 7 % to the supply of services, not provided as part of a social policy, for construction, renovation and alteration of housing, excluding building materials, and to the supply before first occupation of residential buildings or parts of residential buildings, as referred to in Article 12(1)(a).

Article 129

1. [Deleted].

2. Slovenia may, until 31 December 2010, continue to apply a reduced rate of not less than 5 % to the supply of construction, renovation and maintenance work for residential housing not provided as part of a social policy, excluding building materials.

Article 130

[Deleted]

Title IX - Exemptions

Chapter 1 General Provisions

Article 131

The exemptions provided for in Chapters 2 to 9 shall apply without prejudice to other Community provisions and in accordance with conditions which the Member States shall lay down for the purposes of ensuring the correct and straightforward application of those exemptions and of preventing any possible evasion, avoidance or abuse.

Chapter 2 Exemptions for Certain Activities in the Public Interest

Article 132

1. Member States shall exempt the following transactions:

    (a) the supply by the public postal services of services other than passenger transport and telecommunications services, and the supply of goods incidental thereto;

    (b) hospital and medical care and closely related activities undertaken by bodies governed by public law or, under social conditions comparable with those applicable to bodies governed by public law, by hospitals, centers for medical treatment or diagnosis and other duly recognized establishments of a similar nature;

    (c) the provision of medical care in the exercise of the medical and paramedical professions as defined by the Member State concerned;

    (d) the supply of human organs, blood and milk;

    (e) the supply of services by dental technicians in their professional capacity and the supply of dental prostheses by dentists and dental technicians;

    (f) the supply of services by independent groups of persons, who are carrying on an activity which is exempt from VAT or in relation to which they are not taxable persons, for the purpose of rendering their members the services directly necessary for the exercise of that activity, where those groups merely claim from their members exact reimbursement of their share of the joint expenses, provided that such exemption is not likely to cause distortion of competition;

    (g) the supply of services and of goods closely linked to welfare and social security work, including those supplied by old people's homes, by bodies governed by public law or by other bodies recognized by the Member State concerned as being devoted to social wellbeing;

    (h) the supply of services and of goods closely linked to the protection of children and young persons by bodies governed by public law or by other organizations recognized by the Member State concerned as being devoted to social wellbeing;

    (i) the provision of children's or young people's education, school or university education, vocational training or retraining, including the supply of services and of goods closely related thereto, by bodies governed by public law having such as their aim or by other organizations recognized by the Member State concerned as having similar objects;

    (j) tuition given privately by teachers and covering school or university education;

    (k) the supply of staff by religious or philosophical institutions for the purpose of the activities referred to in points (b), (g), (h) and (i) and with a view to spiritual welfare;

    (l) the supply of services, and the supply of goods closely linked thereto, to their members in their common interest in return for a subscription fixed in accordance with their rules by non-profit-making organizations with aims of a political, trade-union, religious, patriotic, philosophical, philanthropic or civic nature, provided that this exemption is not likely to cause distortion of competition;

(m) the supply of certain services closely linked to sport or physical education by non-profit-making organizations to persons taking part in sport or physical education;

(n) the supply of certain cultural services, and the supply of goods closely linked thereto, by bodies governed by public law or by other cultural bodies recognized by the Member State concerned;

(o) the supply of services and goods, by organizations whose activities are exempt pursuant to points (b), (g), (h), (i), (l), (m) and (n), in connection with fund-raising events organized exclusively for their own benefit, provided that exemption is not likely to cause distortion of competition;

(p) the supply of transport services for sick or injured persons in vehicles specially designed for the purpose, by duly authorized bodies;

(q) the activities, other than those of a commercial nature, carried out by public radio and television bodies.

2. For the purposes of point (o) of paragraph 1, Member States may introduce any restrictions necessary, in particular as regards the number of events or the amount of receipts which give entitlement to exemption.

Article 133

Member States may make the granting to bodies other than those governed by public law of each exemption provided for in points (b), (g), (h), (i), (l), (m) and (n) of Article 132(1) subject in each individual case to one or more of the following conditions:

(a) the bodies in question must not systematically aim to make a profit, and any surpluses nevertheless arising must not be distributed, but must be assigned to the continuance or improvement of the services supplied;

(b) those bodies must be managed and administered on an essentially voluntary basis by persons who have no direct or indirect interest, either themselves or through intermediaries, in the results of the activities concerned;

(c) those bodies must charge prices which are approved by the public authorities or which do not exceed such approved prices or, in respect of those services not subject to approval, prices lower than those charged for similar services by commercial enterprises subject to VAT;

(d) the exemptions must not be likely to cause distortion of competition to the disadvantage of commercial enterprises subject to VAT.

Member States which, pursuant to Annex E of Directive 77/388/EEC, on 1 January 1989 applied VAT to the transactions referred to in Article 132(1)(m) and (n) may also apply the conditions provided for in point (d) of the first paragraph of this Article when the said supply of goods or services by bodies governed by public law is granted exemption.

Article 134

The supply of goods or services shall not be granted exemption, as provided for in points (b), (g), (h), (i), (l), (m) and (n) of Article 132(1), in the following cases:

    (a)   where the supply is not essential to the transactions exempted;

    (b)   where the basic purpose of the supply is to obtain additional income for the body in question through transactions which are in direct competition with those of commercial enterprises subject to VAT.

Chapter 3 Exemptions for other Activities

Article 135

1. Member States shall exempt the following transactions:

    (a) insurance and reinsurance transactions, including related services performed by insurance brokers and insurance agents;

    (b) the granting and the negotiation of credit and the management of credit by the person granting it;

    (c) the negotiation of or any dealings in credit guarantees or any other security for money and the management of credit guarantees by the person who is granting the credit;

    (d) transactions, including negotiation, concerning deposit and current accounts, payments, transfers, debts, cheques and other negotiable instruments, but excluding debt collection;

    (e) transactions, including negotiation, concerning currency, bank notes and coins used as legal tender, with the exception of collectors' items, that is to say, gold, silver or other metal coins or bank notes which are not normally used as legal tender or coins of numismatic interest;

    (f) transactions, including negotiation but not management or safekeeping, in shares, interests in companies or associations, debentures and other securities, but excluding documents establishing title to goods, and the rights or securities referred to in Article 15(2);

    (g) the management of special investment funds as defined by Member States;

    (h) the supply at face value of postage stamps valid for use for postal services within their respective territory, fiscal stamps and other similar stamps;

    (i) betting, lotteries and other forms of gambling, subject to the conditions and limitations laid down by each Member State;

    (j) the supply of a building or parts thereof, and of the land on which it stands, other than the supply referred to in point (a) of Article 12(1);

    (k) the supply of land which has not been built on other than the supply of building land as referred to in point (b) of Article 12(1);

    (l) the leasing or letting of immovable property.

2. The following shall be excluded from the exemption provided for in point (l) of paragraph 1:

    (a) the provision of accommodation, as defined in the laws of the Member States, in the hotel sector or in sectors with a similar function, including the provision of accommodation in holiday camps or on sites developed for use as camping sites;

(b) the letting of premises and sites for the parking of vehicles;

(c) the letting of permanently installed equipment and machinery;

(d) the hire of safes.

Member States may apply further exclusions to the scope of the exemption referred to in point (l) of paragraph 1.

Article 136

Member States shall exempt the following transactions:

(a) the supply of goods used solely for an activity exempted under Articles 132, 135, 371, 375, 376 and 377, Article 378(2), Article 379(2) and Articles 380 to 390c, if those goods have not given rise to deductibility;

(b) the supply of goods on the acquisition or application of which VAT was not deductible, pursuant to Article 176.

Article 137

1. Member States may allow taxable persons a right of option for taxation in respect of the following transactions:

    (a) the financial transactions referred to in points (b) to (g) of Article 135(1);

    (b) the supply of a building or of parts thereof, and of the land on which the building stands, other than the supply referred to in point (a) of Article 12(1);

    (c) the supply of land which has not been built on other than the supply of building land referred to in point (b) of Article 12(1);

    (d) the leasing or letting of immovable property.

2. Member States shall lay down the detailed rules governing exercise of the option under paragraph 1.

Member States may restrict the scope of that right of option.

RECAST VAT DIRECTIVE

Chapter 4 Exemptions for Intra-Community Transactions

Section 1: Exemptions related to the Supply of Goods

Article 138

1. Member States shall exempt the supply of goods dispatched or transported to a destination outside their respective territory but within the Community, by or on behalf of the vendor or the person acquiring the goods, for another taxable person, or for a non-taxable legal person acting as such in a Member State other than that in which dispatch or transport of the goods began.

2. In addition to the supply of goods referred to in paragraph 1, Member States shall exempt the following transactions:

    (a) the supply of new means of transport, dispatched or transported to the customer at a destination outside their respective territory but within the Community, by or on behalf of the vendor or the customer, for taxable persons, or non-taxable legal persons, whose intra-Community acquisitions of goods are not subject to VAT pursuant to Article 3(1), or for any other non-taxable person;

    (b) the supply of products subject to excise duty, dispatched or transported to a destination outside their respective territory but within the Community, to the customer, by or on behalf of the vendor or the customer, for taxable persons, or non-taxable legal persons, whose intra-Community acquisitions of goods other than products subject to excise duty are not subject to VAT pursuant to Article 3(1), where those products have been dispatched or transported in accordance with Article 7(4) and (5) or Article 16 of Directive 92/12/EEC;/p>

    (c) the supply of goods, consisting in a transfer to another Member State, which would have been entitled to exemption under paragraph 1 and points (a)>and (b) if it had been made on behalf of another taxable person.

Article 139

1. The exemption provided for in Article 138(1) shall not apply to the supply of goods carried out by taxable persons who are covered by the exemption for small enterprises provided for in Articles 282 to 292.

Nor shall that exemption apply to the supply of goods to taxable persons, or non-taxable legal persons, whose intra-Community acquisitions of goods are not subject to VAT pursuant to Article 3(1).

2. The exemption provided for in Article 138(2)(b) shall not apply to the supply of products subject to excise duty by taxable persons who are covered by the exemption for small enterprises provided for in Articles 282 to 292.

3. The exemption provided for in Article 138(1) and (2)(b) and (c) shall not apply to the supply of goods subject to VAT in accordance with the margin scheme provided for in Articles 312 to 325 or the special arrangements for sales by public auction.

The exemption provided for in Article 138(1) and (2)(c) shall not apply to the supply of second-hand means of transport, as defined in Article 327(3), subject to VAT in accordance with the transitional arrangements for second-hand means of transport.

Section 2 Exemptions for Intra-Community Acquisitions of Goods

Article 140

Member States shall exempt the following transactions:

(a) the intra-Community acquisition of goods the supply of which by taxable persons would in all circumstances be exempt within their respective territory;

(b) the intra-Community acquisition of goods the importation of which would in all circumstances be exempt under points (a), (b) and (c) and (e) to (l) of Article 143(1)

(c) the intra-Community acquisition of goods where, pursuant to Articles 170 and 171, the person acquiring the goods would in all circumstances be entitled to full reimbursement of the VAT due under Article 2(1)(b).

Article 141

Each Member State shall take specific measures to ensure that VAT is not charged on the intra-Community acquisition of goods within its territory, made in accordance with Article 40, where the following conditions are met:

(a) the acquisition of goods is made by a taxable person who is not established in the Member State concerned but is identified for VAT purposes in another Member State;

(b) the acquisition of goods is made for the purposes of the subsequent supply of those goods, in the Member State concerned, by the taxable person referred to in point (a);

(c) the goods thus acquired by the taxable person referred to in point (a) are directly dispatched or transported, from a Member State other than that in which he is identified for VAT purposes, to the person for whom he is to carry out the subsequent supply;

(d) the person to whom the subsequent supply is to be made is another taxable person, or a non-taxable legal person, who is identified for VAT purposes in the Member State concerned;

(e) the person referred to in point (d) has been designated in accordance with Article 197 as liable for payment of the VAT due on the supply carried out by the taxable person who is not established in the Member State in which the tax is due.

Section 3 Exemptions for Certain Transport Services

Article 142

Member States shall exempt the supply of intra-Community transport of goods to and from the islands making up the autonomous regions of the Azores and Madeira, as well as the supply of transport of goods between those islands.

Chapter 5: Exemptions on Importation

Article 143

1. Member States shall exempt the following transactions:

    (a) the final importation of goods of which the supply by a taxable person would in all circumstances be exempt within their respective territory;

    (b) the final importation of goods governed by Council Directives 69/169/EEC, 83/181/EEC and 2006/79/EC;

    (c) the final importation of goods, in free circulation from a third territory forming part of the Community customs territory, which would be entitled to exemption under point (b) if they had been imported within the meaning of the first paragraph of Article 30;

    (d) the importation of goods dispatched or transported from a third territory or a third country into a Member State other than that in which the dispatch or transport of the goods ends, where the supply of such goods by the importer designated or recognized under Article 201 as liable for payment of VAT is exempt under Article 138;

    (e) the reimportation, by the person who exported them, of goods in the state in which they were exported, where those goods are exempt from customs duties;

    (f) the importation, under diplomatic and consular arrangements, of goods which are exempt from customs duties;

    (fa) the importation of goods by the European Community, the European Atomic Energy Community, the European Central Bank or the European Investment Bank, or by the bodies set up by the Communities to which the Protocol of 8 April 1965 on the privileges and immunities of the European Communities applies, within the limits and under the conditions of that Protocol and the agreements for its implementation or the headquarters agreements, in so far as it does not lead to distortion of competition;

    (g) the importation of goods by international bodies, other than those referred to in point (fa), recognized as such by the public authorities of the host Member State, or by members of such bodies, within the limits and under the conditions laid down by the international conventions establishing the bodies or by headquarters agreements;

    (h) the importation of goods, into Member States party to the North Atlantic Treaty, by the armed forces of other States party to that Treaty for the use of those forces or the civilian staff accompanying them or for supplying their messes or canteens where such forces take part in the common defense effort;

    (i) the importation of goods by the armed forces of the United Kingdom stationed in the island of Cyprus pursuant to the Treaty of Establishment concerning the Republic of Cyprus, dated 16 August 1960, which are for the use of those forces or the civilian staff accompanying them or for supplying their messes or canteens;

(j) the importation into ports, by sea fishing undertakings, of their catches, unprocessed or after undergoing preservation for marketing but before being supplied;

(k) the importation of gold by central banks;

(l) the importation of gas through a natural gas system or any network connected to such a system or fed in from a vessel transporting gas into a natural gas system or any upstream pipeline network, of electricity or of heat or cooling energy through heating or cooling networks.

2. The exemption provided for in paragraph 1(d) shall apply in cases when the importation of goods is followed by the supply of goods exempted under Article 138(1) and (2)(c) only if at the time of importation the importer has provided to the competent authorities of the Member State of importation at least the following information:

(a) his VAT identification number issued in the Member State of importation or the VAT identification number of his tax representative, liable for payment of the VAT, issued in the Member State of importation;

(b) the VAT identification number of the customer, to whom the goods are supplied in accordance with Article 138(1), issued in another Member State, or his own VAT identification number issued in the Member State in which the dispatch or transport of the goods ends when the goods are subject to a transfer in accordance with Article 138(2)(c);

(c) the evidence that the imported goods are intended to be transported or dispatched from the Member State of importation to another Member State.

However, Member States may provide that the evidence referred to in point (c) be indicated to the competent authorities only upon request.

Article 144

Member States shall exempt the supply of services relating to the importation of goods where the value of such services is included in the taxable amount in accordance with Article 86(1)(b).

Article 145

1. The Commission shall, where appropriate, as soon as possible, present to the Council proposals designed to delimit the scope of the exemptions provided for in Articles 143 and 144 and to lay down the detailed rules for their implementation.

2. Pending the entry into force of the rules referred to in paragraph 1, Member States may maintain their national provisions in force.

Member States may adapt their national provisions so as to minimize distortion of competition and, in particular, to prevent non-taxation or double taxation within the Community.

Member States may use whatever administrative procedures they consider most appropriate to achieve exemption.

3. Member States shall notify to the Commission, which shall inform the other Member States accordingly, the provisions of national law which are in force, in so far as these have not already been notified, and those which they adopt pursuant to paragraph 2.

Chapter 6 Exemptions on Exportation

Article 146

1. Member States shall exempt the following transactions:

    (a) the supply of goods dispatched or transported to a destination outside the Community by or on behalf of the vendor;

    (b) the supply of goods dispatched or transported to a destination outside the Community by or on behalf of a customer not established within their respective territory, with the exception of goods transported by the customer himself for the equipping, fuelling and provisioning of pleasure boats and private aircraft or any other means of transport for private use;

    (c) the supply of goods to approved bodies which export them out of the Community as part of their humanitarian, charitable or teaching activities outside the Community;

    (d) the supply of services consisting in work on movable property acquired or imported for the purpose of undergoing such work within the Community, and dispatched or transported out of the Community by the supplier, by the customer if not established within their respective territory or on behalf of either of them;

    (e) the supply of services, including transport and ancillary transactions, but excluding the supply of services exempted in accordance with Articles 132 and 135, where these are directly connected with the exportation or importation of goods covered by Article 61 and Article 157(1)(a).

2. The exemption provided for in point (c) of paragraph 1 may be granted by means of a refund of the VAT.

Article 147

1. Where the supply of goods referred to in point (b) of Article 146(1) relates to goods to be carried in the personal luggage of travelers, the exemption shall apply only if the following conditions are met:

    (a) the traveler is not established within the Community;

    (b) the goods are transported out of the Community before the end of the third month following that in which the supply takes place;

    (c) the total value of the supply, including VAT, is more than EUR 175 or the equivalent in national currency, fixed annually by applying the conversion rate obtaining on the first working day of October with effect from 1 January of the following year.

However, Member States may exempt a supply with a total value of less than the amount specified in point (c) of the first subparagraph.

2. For the purposes of paragraph 1, "a traveler who is not established within the Community" shall mean a traveler whose permanent address or habitual residence is not located within the Community. In that case "permanent address or habitual residence" means the place entered as such in a passport, identity card or other document recognized as an identity document by the Member State within whose territory the supply takes place.

Proof of exportation shall be furnished by means of the invoice or other document in lieu thereof, endorsed by the customs office of exit from the Community.

Each Member State shall send to the Commission specimens of the stamps it uses for the endorsement referred to in the second subparagraph. The Commission shall forward that information to the tax authorities of the other Member States.

Chapter 7 Exemptions Related to International Transport

Article 148

Member States shall exempt the following transactions:

(a) the supply of goods for the fuelling and provisioning of vessels used for navigation on the high seas and carrying passengers for reward or used for the purpose of commercial, industrial or fishing activities, or for rescue or assistance at sea, or for inshore fishing, with the exception, in the case of vessels used for inshore fishing, of ships' provisions;

(b) the supply of goods for the fuelling and provisioning of fighting ships, falling within the combined nomenclature (CN) code 8906 10 00, leaving their territory and bound for ports or anchorages outside the Member State concerned;

(c) the supply, modification, repair, maintenance, chartering and hiring of the vessels referred to in point (a) and the supply, hiring, repair and maintenance of equipment, including fishing equipment, incorporated or used therein;

(d) the supply of services other than those referred to in point (c), to meet the direct needs of the vessels referred to in point (a) or of their cargoes;

(e) the supply of goods for the fuelling and provisioning of aircraft used by airlines operating for reward chiefly on international routes;

(f) the supply, modification, repair, maintenance, chartering and hiring of the aircraft referred to in point (e), and the supply, hiring, repair and maintenance of equipment incorporated or used therein;

(g) the supply of services, other than those referred to in point (f), to meet the direct needs of the aircraft referred to in point (e) or of their cargoes.

Article 149

Portugal may treat sea and air transport between the islands making up the autonomous regions of the Azores and Madeira and between those regions and the mainland as international transport.

Article 150

1. The Commission shall, where appropriate, as soon as possible, present to the Council proposals designed to delimit the scope of the exemptions provided for in Article 148 and to lay down the detailed rules for their implementation.

2. Pending the entry into force of the provisions referred to in paragraph 1, Member States may limit the scope of the exemptions provided for in points (a) and (b) of Article 148.

Chapter 8 Exemptions Relating to Certain Transactions treated as Exports

Article 151

1. Member States shall exempt the following transactions:

    (a) the supply of goods or services under diplomatic and consular arrangements;

    (aa) the supply of goods or services to the European Community, the European Atomic Energy Community, the European Central Bank or the European Investment Bank, or to the bodies set up by the Communities to which the Protocol of 8 April 1965 on the privileges and immunities of the European Communities applies, within the limits and under the conditions of that Protocol and the agreements for its implementation or the headquarters agreements, in so far as it does not lead to distortion of competition;

    (b) the supply of goods or services to international bodies, other than those referred to in point (aa), recognized as such by the public authorities of the host Member States, and to members of such bodies, within the limits and under the conditions laid down by the international conventions establishing the bodies or by headquarters agreements;

    (c) the supply of goods or services within a Member State which is a party to the North Atlantic Treaty, intended either for the armed forces of other States party to that Treaty for the use of those forces, or of the civilian staff accompanying them, or for supplying their messes or canteens when such forces take part in the common defense effort;

    (d) the supply of goods or services to another Member State, intended for the armed forces of any State which is a party to the North Atlantic Treaty, other than the Member State of destination itself, for the use of those forces, or of the civilian staff accompanying them, or for supplying their messes or canteens when such forces take part in the common defense effort;

    (e) the supply of goods or services to the armed forces of the United Kingdom stationed in the island of Cyprus pursuant to the Treaty of Establishment concerning the Republic of Cyprus, dated 16 August 1960, which are for the use of those forces, or of the civilian staff accompanying them, or for supplying their messes or canteens.

    Pending the adoption of common tax rules, the exemptions provided for in the first subparagraph shall be subject to the limitations laid down by the host Member State.

2. In cases where the goods are not dispatched or transported out of the Member State in which the supply takes place, and in the case of services, the exemption may be granted by means of a refund of the VAT.

Article 152

Member States shall exempt the supply of gold to central banks.

Chapter 9 Exemptions for the Supply of Services by Intermediaries

Article 153

Member States shall exempt the supply of services by intermediaries, acting in the name and on behalf of another person, where they take part in the transactions referred to in Chapters 6, 7 and 8, or of transactions carried out outside the Community.

The exemption referred to in the first paragraph shall not apply to travel agents who, in the name and on behalf of travelers, supply services which are carried out in other Member States.

Chapter 10 Exemptions for Transactions relating to International Trade

Section 1: Customs warehouses, warehouses other than customs warehouses and similar arrangements

Article 154

For the purposes of this Section, "warehouses other than customs warehouses" shall, in the case of products subject to excise duty, mean the places defined as tax warehouses by Article 4(b) of Directive 92/12/EEC and, in the case of products not subject to excise duty, the places defined as such by the Member States.

Article 155

Without prejudice to other Community tax provisions, Member States may, after consulting the VAT Committee, take special measures designed to exempt all or some of the transactions referred to in this Section, provided that those measures are not aimed at final use or consumption and that the amount of VAT due on cessation of the arrangements or situations referred to in this Section corresponds to the amount of tax which would have been due had each of those transactions been taxed within their territory.

Article 156

1. Member States may exempt the following transactions:

    (a) the supply of goods which are intended to be presented to customs and, where applicable, placed in temporary storage;

    (b) the supply of goods which are intended to be placed in a free zone or in a free warehouse;

(c) the supply of goods which are intended to be placed under customs warehousing arrangements or inward processing arrangements;

(d) the supply of goods which are intended to be admitted into territorial waters in order to be incorporated into drilling or production platforms, for purposes of the construction, repair, maintenance, alteration or fitting-out of such platforms, or to link such drilling or production platforms to the mainland;

(e) the supply of goods which are intended to be admitted into territorial waters for the fuelling and provisioning of drilling or production platforms.

2. The places referred to in paragraph 1 shall be those defined as such by the Community customs provisions in force.

Article 157

1. Member States may exempt the following transactions:

    (a) the importation of goods which are intended to be placed under warehousing arrangements other than customs warehousing;

    (b) the supply of goods which are intended to be placed, within their territory, under warehousing arrangements other than customs warehousing.

2. Member States may not provide for warehousing arrangements other than customs warehousing for goods which are not subject to excise duty where those goods are intended to be supplied at the retail stage.

Article 158

1. By way of derogation from Article 157(2), Member States may provide for warehousing arrangements other than customs warehousing in the following cases:

    (a) where the goods are intended for tax-free shops, for the purposes of the supply of goods to be carried in the personal luggage of travelers taking flights or sea crossings to third territories or third countries, where that supply is exempt pursuant to point (b) of Article 146(1);

    (b) where the goods are intended for taxable persons, for the purposes of carrying out supplies to travelers on board an aircraft or a ship in the course of a flight or sea crossing where the place of arrival is situated outside the Community;

    (c) where the goods are intended for taxable persons, for the purposes of carrying out supplies which are exempt from VAT pursuant to Article 151.

2. Where Member States exercise the option of exemption provided for in point (a) of paragraph 1, they shall take the measures necessary to ensure the correct and straightforward application of this exemption and to prevent any evasion, avoidance or abuse.

3. For the purposes of point (a) of paragraph 1, "tax-free shop" shall mean any establishment which is situated within an airport or port and which fulfils the conditions laid down by the competent public authorities.

Article 159

Member States may exempt the supply of services relating to the supply of goods referred to in Article 156, Article 157(1)(b) or Article 158.

Article 160

1. Member States may exempt the following transactions:

    (a) the supply of goods or services carried out in the locations referred to in Article 156(1), where one of the situations specified therein still applies within their territory;

    (b) the supply of goods or services carried out in the locations referred to in Article 157(1)(b) or Article 158, where one of the situations specified in Article 157(1)(b) or in Article 158(1) still applies within their territory.

2. Where Member States exercise the option under point (a) of paragraph 1 in respect of transactions effected in customs warehouses, they shall take the measures necessary to provide for warehousing arrangements other than customs warehousing under which point (b) of paragraph 1 may be applied to the same transactions when they concern goods listed in Annex V and are carried out in warehouses other than customs warehouses.

Article 161

Member States may exempt supply of the following goods and of services relating thereto:

(a) the supply of goods referred to in the first paragraph of Article 30 while they remain covered by arrangements for temporary importation with total exemption from import duty or by external transit arrangements;

(b) the supply of goods referred to in the second paragraph of Article 30 while they remain covered by the internal Community transit procedure referred to in Article 276.

Article 162

Where Member States exercise the option provided for in this Section, they shall take the measures necessary to ensure that the intra-Community acquisition of goods intended to be placed under one of the arrangements or in one of the situations referred to in Article 156, Article 157(1)(b) or Article 158 is covered by the same provisions as the supply of goods carried out within their territory under the same conditions.

Article 163

If the goods cease to be covered by the arrangements or situations referred to in this Section, thus giving rise to importation for the purposes of Article 61, the Member State of importation shall take the measures necessary to prevent double taxation.

Section 2: Transactions exempted with a view to export and in the framework of trade between the Member States

Article 164

1. Member States may, after consulting the VAT Committee, exempt the following transactions carried out by, or intended for, a taxable person up to an amount equal to the value of the exports carried out by that person during the preceding 12 months:

   (a) intra-Community acquisitions of goods made by the taxable person, and imports for and supplies of goods to the taxable person, with a view to their exportation from the Community as they are or after processing;

   (b) supplies of services linked with the export business of the taxable person.

2. Where Member States exercise the option of exemption under paragraph 1, they shall, after consulting the VAT Committee, apply that exemption also to transactions relating to supplies carried out by the taxable person, in accordance with the conditions specified in Article 138, up to an amount equal to the value of the supplies carried out by that person, in accordance with the same conditions, during the preceding 12 months.

Article 165

Member States may set a common maximum amount for transactions which they exempt pursuant to Article 164.

Section 3: Provisions common to Sections 1 and 2

Article 166

The Commission shall, where appropriate, as soon as possible, present to the Council proposals concerning common arrangements for applying VAT to the transactions referred to in Sections 1 and 2.

Title X Deductions

Chapter 1 Origin and Scope of Right of Deduction

Article 167

A right of deduction shall arise at the time the deductible tax becomes chargeable.

Article 167a

Member States may provide within an optional scheme that the right of deduction of a taxable person whose VAT solely becomes chargeable in accordance with Article 66(b) be postponed until the VAT on the goods or services supplied to him has been paid to his supplier.

Member States which apply the optional scheme referred to in the first paragraph shall set a threshold for taxable persons using the scheme within their territory, based on the annual turnover of the taxable person calculated in accordance with Article 288. That threshold may not be higher than EUR 500,000 or the equivalent in national currency. Member States may increase that threshold up to EUR 200,0000 or the equivalent in national currency after consulting the VAT Committee. However, such consultation of the VAT Committee shall not be required for Member States which applied a threshold higher than EUR 500,000 or the equivalent in national currency on 31 December 2012.

Member States shall inform the VAT Committee of national legislative measures adopted pursuant to the first paragraph.

Article 168

In so far as the goods and services are used for the purposes of the taxed transactions of a taxable person, the taxable person shall be entitled, in the Member State in which he carries out these transactions, to deduct the following from the VAT which he is liable to pay:

- (a) the VAT due or paid in that Member State in respect of supplies to him of goods or services, carried out or to be carried out by another taxable person;
- (b) the VAT due in respect of transactions treated as supplies of goods or services pursuant to Article 18 (a)and Article 27;
- (c) the VAT due in respect of intra-Community acquisitions of goods pursuant to Article 2(1)(b)(i);
- (d) the VAT due on transactions treated as intra-Community acquisitions in accordance with Articles 21 and 22;
- (e) the VAT due or paid in respect of the importation of goods into that Member State.

Article 168a

1. In the case of immovable property forming part of the business assets of a taxable person and used both for purposes of the taxable person's business and for his private use or that of his staff, or, more generally, for purposes other than those of his business, VAT on expenditure related to this property shall be deductible in accordance with the principles set out in Articles 167, 168, 169 and 173 only up to the proportion of the property's use for purposes of the taxable person's business.

By way of derogation from Article 26, changes in the proportion of use of immovable property referred to in the first subparagraph shall be taken into account in accordance with the principles provided for in Articles 184 to 192 as applied in the respective Member State.

2. Member States may also apply paragraph 1 in relation to VAT on expenditure related to other goods forming part of the business assets as they specify.

Article 169

In addition to the deduction referred to in Article 168, the taxable person shall be entitled to deduct the VAT referred to therein in so far as the goods and services are used for the purposes of the following:

(a) transactions relating to the activities referred to in the second subparagraph of Article 9(1), carried out outside the Member State in which that tax is due or paid, in respect of which VAT would be deductible if they had been carried out within that Member State;

(b) transactions which are exempt pursuant to Articles 138, 142 or 144, Articles 146 to 149, Articles 151, 152, 153 or 156, Article 157(1)(b), Articles 158 to 161 or Article 164;

(c) transactions which are exempt pursuant to points (a) to (f) of Article 135(1), where the customer is established outside the Community or where those transactions relate directly to goods to be exported out of the Community.

Article 170

All taxable persons who, within the meaning of Article 1 of Directive 86/560/EEC, Article 2(1) and Article 3 of Directive 2008/9/EC and Article 171 of this Directive, are not established in the Member State in which they purchase goods and services or import goods subject to VAT shall be entitled to obtain a refund of that VAT insofar as the goods and services are used for the purposes of the following:

(a) transactions referred to in Article 169;

(b) transactions for which the tax is solely payable by the customer in accordance with Articles 194 to 197 or Article 199.

Article 171

1. VAT shall be refunded to taxable persons who are not established in the Member State in which they purchase goods and services or import goods subject to VAT but

who are established in another Member State, in accordance with the detailed rules laid down in Directive 2008/9/EC.

2. VAT shall be refunded to taxable persons who are not established within the territory of the Community in accordance with the detailed implementing rules laid down in Directive 86/560/EEC.

The taxable persons referred to in Article 1 of Directive 86/560/EEC shall also, for the purposes of applying that Directive, be regarded as taxable persons who are not established in the Community where, in the Member State in which they purchase goods and services or import goods subject to VAT, they have only carried out the supply of goods or services to a person designated in accordance with Articles 194 to 197 or Article 199 as liable for payment of VAT.

3. Directive 86/560/EEC shall not apply to:

    (a) amounts of VAT which according to the legislation of the Member State of refund have been incorrectly invoiced;

    (b) invoiced amounts of VAT in respect of supplies of goods the supply of which is, or may be, exempt pursuant to Article 138 or Article 146(1)(b).

Article 171a

Member States may, instead of granting a refund of VAT pursuant to Directives 86/560/EEC or 2008/9/EC on those supplies of goods or services to a taxable person in respect of which the taxable person is liable to pay the tax in accordance with Articles 194 to 197 or Article 199, allow deduction of this tax pursuant to the procedure laid down in Article 168. The existing restrictions pursuant to Article 2(2) and Article 4(2) of Directive 86/560/EEC may be retained.

To that end, Member States may exclude the taxable person who is liable to pay the tax from the refund procedure pursuant to Directives 86/560/EEC or 2008/9/EC.

Article 172

1. Any person who is regarded as a taxable person by reason of the fact that he supplies, on an occasional basis, a new means of transport in accordance with the conditions specified in Article 138(1) and (2)(a) shall, in the Member State in which the supply takes place, be entitled to deduct the VAT included in the purchase price or paid in respect of the importation or the intra-Community acquisition of this means of transport, up to an amount not exceeding the amount of VAT for which he would be liable if the supply were not exempt.

A right of deduction shall arise and may be exercised only at the time of supply of the new means of transport.

2. Member States shall lay down detailed rules for the implementation of paragraph 1.

Chapter 2 Proportional Deduction

Article 173

1. In the case of goods or services used by a taxable person both for transactions in respect of which VAT is deductible pursuant to Articles 168, 169 and 170, and for transactions in respect of which VAT is not deductible, only such proportion of the VAT as is attributable to the former transactions shall be deductible.

The deductible proportion shall be determined, in accordance with Articles 174 and 175, for all the transactions carried out by the taxable person.

2. Member States may take the following measures:

    (a) authorize the taxable person to determine a proportion for each sector of his business, provided that separate accounts are kept for each sector;

    (b) require the taxable person to determine a proportion for each sector of his business and to keep separate accounts for each sector;

    (c) authorize or require the taxable person to make the deduction on the basis of the use made of all or part of the goods and services;

    (d) authorize or require the taxable person to make the deduction in accordance with the rule laid down in the first subparagraph of paragraph 1, in respect of all goods and services used for all transactions referred to therein;

    (e) provide that, where the VAT which is not deductible by the taxable person is insignificant, it is to be treated as nil.

Article 174

1. The deductible proportion shall be made up of a fraction comprising the following amounts:

    (a) as numerator, the total amount, exclusive of VAT, of turnover per year attributable to transactions in respect of which VAT is deductible pursuant to Articles 168 and 169;

    (b) as denominator, the total amount, exclusive of VAT, of turnover per year attributable to transactions included in the numerator and to transactions in respect of which VAT is not deductible.

2. Member States may include in the denominator the amount of subsidies, other than those directly linked to the price of supplies of goods or services referred to in Article 73.

3. By way of derogation from paragraph 1, the following amounts shall be excluded from the calculation of the deductible proportion:

    (a) the amount of turnover attributable to supplies of capital goods used by the taxable person for the purposes of his business;

(b) the amount of turnover attributable to incidental real estate and financial transactions;

(c) the amount of turnover attributable to the transactions specified in points (b) to (g) of Article 135(1) in so far as those transactions are incidental.

4. 3 Where Member States exercise the option under Article 191 not to require adjustment in respect of capital goods, they may include disposals of capital goods in the calculation of the deductible proportion.

Article 175

1. The deductible proportion shall be determined on an annual basis, fixed as a percentage and rounded up to a figure not exceeding the next whole number.

2. The provisional proportion for a year shall be that calculated on the basis of the preceding year's transactions. In the absence of any such transactions to refer to, or where they were insignificant in amount, the deductible proportion shall be estimated provisionally, under the supervision of the tax authorities, by the taxable person on the basis of his own forecasts.

However, Member States may retain the rules in force at 1 January 1979 or, in the case of the Member States which acceded to the Community after that date, on the date of their accession.

3. Deductions made on the basis of such provisional proportions shall be adjusted when the final proportion is fixed during the following year.

Chapter 3 Restrictions on the Right of Deduction

Article 176

The Council, acting unanimously on a proposal from the Commission, shall determine the expenditure in respect of which VAT shall not be deductible. VAT shall in no circumstances be deductible in respect of expenditure which is not strictly business expenditure, such as that on luxuries, amusements or entertainment.

Pending the entry into force of the provisions referred to in the first paragraph, Member States may retain all the exclusions provided for under their national laws at 1 January 1979 or, in the case of the Member States which acceded to the Community after that date, on the date of their accession.

Article 177

After consulting the VAT Committee, each Member State may, for cyclical economic reasons, totally or partly exclude all or some capital goods or other goods from the system of deductions.

In order to maintain identical conditions of competition, Member States may, instead of refusing deduction, tax goods manufactured by the taxable person himself or goods which he has purchased within the Community, or imported, in such a way that the tax does not exceed the amount of VAT which would be charged on the acquisition of similar goods.

Chapter 4 Rules Governing Exercise of the Right of Deduction

Article 178

In order to exercise the right of deduction, a taxable person must meet the following conditions:

(a) for the purposes of deductions pursuant to Article 168(a), in respect of the supply of goods or services, he must hold an invoice drawn up in accordance with Sections 3 to 6 of Chapter 3 of Title XI;

(b) for the purposes of deductions pursuant to Article 168(b), in respect of transactions treated as the supply of goods or services, he must comply with the formalities as laid down by each Member State;

(c) for the purposes of deductions pursuant to Article 168(c), in respect of the intra-Community acquisition of goods, he must set out in the VAT return provided for in Article 250 all the information needed for the amount of VAT due on his intra-Community acquisitions of goods to be calculated and he must hold an invoice drawn up in accordance with Sections 3 to 5 of Chapter 3 of Title XI;

(d) for the purposes of deductions pursuant to Article 168(d), in respect of transactions treated as intra-Community acquisitions of goods, he must complete the formalities as laid down by each Member State;

(e) for the purposes of deductions pursuant to Article 168(e), in respect of the importation of goods, he must hold an import document specifying him as consignee or importer, and stating the amount of VAT due or enabling that amount to be calculated;

(f) when required to pay VAT as a customer where Articles 194 to 197 or Article 199 apply, he must comply with the formalities as laid down by each Member State.

Article 179

The taxable person shall make the deduction by subtracting from the total amount of VAT due for a given tax period the total amount of VAT in respect of which, during the same period, the right of deduction has arisen and is exercised in accordance with Article 178.

However, Member States may require that taxable persons who carry out occasional transactions, as defined in Article 12, exercise their right of deduction only at the time of supply.

Article 180

Member States may authorize a taxable person to make a deduction which he has not made in accordance with Articles 178 and 179.

Article 181

Member States may authorize a taxable person who does not hold an invoice drawn up in accordance with Sections 3 to 5 of Chapter 3 of Title XI to make the deduction referred to in Article 168(c) in respect of his intra-Community acquisitions of goods.

Article 182

Member States shall determine the conditions and detailed rules for applying Articles 180 and 181.

Article 183

Where, for a given tax period, the amount of deductions exceeds the amount of VAT due, the Member States may, in accordance with conditions which they shall determine, either make a refund or carry the excess forward to the following period.

However, Member States may refuse to refund or carry forward if the amount of the excess is insignificant.

Chapter 5 Adjustment of Deductions

Article 184

The initial deduction shall be adjusted where it is higher or lower than that to which the taxable person was entitled.

Article 185

1. Adjustment shall, in particular, be made where, after the VAT return is made, some change occurs in the factors used to determine the amount to be deducted, for example where purchases are cancelled or price reductions are obtained.

2. By way of derogation from paragraph 1, no adjustment shall be made in the case of transactions remaining totally or partially unpaid or in the case of destruction, loss or theft of property duly proved or confirmed, or in the case of goods reserved for the purpose of making gifts of small value or of giving samples, as referred to in Article 16.

However, in the case of transactions remaining totally or partially unpaid or in the case of theft, Member States may require adjustment to be made.

Article 186

Member States shall lay down the detailed rules for applying Articles 184 and 185.

Article 187

1. In the case of capital goods, adjustment shall be spread over five years including that in which the goods were acquired or manufactured.

Member States may, however, base the adjustment on a period of five full years starting from the time at which the goods are first used.

In the case of immovable property acquired as capital goods, the adjustment period may be extended up to 20 years.

2. The annual adjustment shall be made only in respect of one-fifth of the VAT charged on the capital goods, or, if the adjustment period has been extended, in respect of the corresponding fraction thereof.

The adjustment referred to in the first subparagraph shall be made on the basis of the variations in the deduction entitlement in subsequent years in relation to that for the year in which the goods were acquired, manufactured or, where applicable, used for the first time.

Article 188

1. If supplied during the adjustment period, capital goods shall be treated as if they had been applied to an economic activity of the taxable person up until expiry of the adjustment period.

   The economic activity shall be presumed to be fully taxed in cases where the supply of the capital goods is taxed.

   The economic activity shall be presumed to be fully exempt in cases where the supply of the capital goods is exempt.

2. The adjustment provided for in paragraph 1 shall be made only once in respect of all the time covered by the adjustment period that remains to run. However, where the supply of capital goods is exempt, Member States may waive the requirement for adjustment in so far as the purchaser is a taxable person using the capital goods in question solely for transactions in respect of which VAT is deductible.

Article 189

For the purposes of applying Articles 187 and 188, Member States may take the following measures:

   (a) define the concept of capital goods;

   (b) specify the amount of the VAT which is to be taken into consideration for adjustment;

   (c) adopt any measures needed to ensure that adjustment does not give rise to any unjustified advantage;

   (d) permit administrative simplifications.

Article 190

For the purposes of Articles 187, 188, 189 and 191, Member States may regard as capital goods those services which have characteristics similar to those normally attributed to capital goods.

Article 191

If, in any Member State, the practical effect of applying Articles 187 and 188 is negligible, that Member State may, after consulting the VAT Committee, refrain from applying those provisions, having regard to the overall impact of VAT in the Member State concerned and the need for administrative simplification, and provided that no distortion of competition thereby arises.

Article 192

Where a taxable person transfers from being taxed in the normal way to a special scheme or vice versa, Member States may take all measures necessary to ensure that the taxable person does not enjoy unjustified advantage or sustain unjustified harm.

Title XI - Obligations of Taxable Persons and Certain Non-Taxable Persons

Chapter 1 Obligation to Pay

Section 1 Persons liable for payment of VAT to the tax authorities

Article 192a

For the purposes of this Section, a taxable person who has a fixed establishment within the territory of the Member State where the tax is due shall be regarded as a taxable person who is not established within that Member State when the following conditions are met:

(a) he makes a taxable supply of goods or of services within the territory of that Member State;

(b) an establishment which the supplier has within the territory of that Member State does not intervene in that supply.

Article 193

VAT shall be payable by any taxable person carrying out a taxable supply of goods or services, except where it is payable by another person in the cases referred to in Articles 194 to 199b and Article 202.

Article 194

1. Where the taxable supply of goods or services is carried out by a taxable person who is not established in the Member State in which the VAT is due, Member States may provide that the person liable for payment of VAT is the person to whom the goods or services are supplied.

2. Member States shall lay down the conditions for implementation of paragraph 1.

Article 195

VAT shall be payable by any person who is identified for VAT purposes in the Member State in which the tax is due and to whom goods are supplied in the circumstances specified in Articles 38 or 39, if the supplies are carried out by a taxable person not established within that Member State.

Article 196

VAT shall be payable by any taxable person, or non-taxable legal person identified for VAT purposes, to whom the services referred to in Article 44 are supplied, if the services are supplied by a taxable person not established within the territory of the Member State.

Article 197

1. VAT shall be payable by the person to whom the goods are supplied when the following conditions are met:

    (a) the taxable transaction is a supply of goods carried out in accordance with the conditions laid down in Article 141;

    (b) the person to whom the goods are supplied is another taxable person, or a non-taxable legal person, identified for VAT purposes in the Member State in which the supply is carried out;

    (c) the invoice issued by the taxable person not established in the Member State of the person to whom the goods are supplied is drawn up in accordance with Sections 3 to 5 of Chapter 3.

2. Where a tax representative is appointed as the person liable for payment of VAT pursuant to Article 204, Member States may provide for a derogation from paragraph 1 of this Article.

Article 198

1. Where specific transactions relating to investment gold between a taxable person who is a member of a regulated gold bullion market and another taxable person who is not a member of that market are taxed pursuant to Article 352, Member States shall designate the customer as the person liable for payment of VAT.

If the customer who is not a member of the regulated gold bullion market is a taxable person required to be identified for VAT purposes in the Member State in which the tax is due solely in respect of the transactions referred to in Article 352, the vendor shall fulfill the tax obligations on behalf of the customer, in accordance with the law of that Member State.

2. Where gold material or semi-manufactured products of a purity of 325 thousandths or greater, or investment gold as defined in Article 344(1) is supplied by a taxable person exercising one of the options under Articles 348, 349 and 350, Member States may designate the customer as the person liable for payment of VAT.

3. Member States shall lay down the procedures and conditions for implementation of paragraphs 1 and 2.

Article 199

1. Member States may provide that the person liable for payment of VAT is the taxable person to whom any of the following supplies are made:

    (a) the supply of construction work, including repair, cleaning, maintenance, alteration and demolition services in relation to immovable property, as well as the handing over of construction works regarded as a supply of goods pursuant to Article 14(3);

(b) the supply of staff engaged in activities covered by point (a);

(c) the supply of immovable property, as referred to in Article 135(1)(j) and (k), where the supplier has opted for taxation of the supply pursuant to Article 137;

(d) the supply of used material, used material which cannot be re-used in the same state, scrap, industrial and non industrial waste, recyclable waste, part processed waste and certain goods and services, as listed in Annex VI;

(e) the supply of goods provided as security by one taxable person to another in execution of that security;

(f) the supply of goods following the cession of a reservation of ownership to an assignee and the exercising of this right by the assignee;

(g) the supply of immovable property sold by a judgment debtor in a compulsory sale procedure.

2. When applying the option provided for in paragraph 1, Member States may specify the supplies of goods and services covered, and the categories of suppliers or recipients to whom these measures may apply.

3. For the purposes of paragraph 1, Member States may take the following measures:

(a) provide that a taxable person who also carries out activities or transactions that are not considered to be taxable supplies of goods or services in accordance with Article 2 shall be regarded as a taxable person in respect of supplies received as referred to in paragraph 1 of this Article;

(b) provide that a non-taxable body governed by public law, shall be regarded as a taxable person in respect of supplies received as referred to in points (e), (f) and (g) of paragraph 1.

4. Member States shall inform the VAT Committee of national legislative measures adopted pursuant to paragraph 1 in so far as these are not measures authorized by the Council prior to 13 August 2006 in accordance with Article 27(1) to (4) of Directive 77/388/EEC, and which are continued under paragraph 1 of this Article.

Article 199a

1. Member States may, until 31 December 2018 and for a minimum period of two years, provide that the person liable for payment of VAT is the taxable person to whom any of the following supplies are made

(a) the transfer of allowances to emit greenhouse gases as defined in Article 3 of Directive 2003/87/EC of the European Parliament and of the Council of 13 October 2003 establishing a scheme for greenhouse gas emission allowance trading within the Community, transferable in accordance with Article 12 of that Directive;

(b) the transfer of other units that may be used by operators for compliance with the same Directive.

(c) supplies of mobile telephones, being devices made or adapted for use in connection with a licensed network and operated on specified frequencies, whether or not they have any other use;

(d) supplies of integrated circuit devices such as microprocessors and central processing units in a state prior to integration into end user products;

(e) supplies of gas and electricity to a taxable dealer as defined in Article 38(2);

(f) supplies of gas and electricity certificates;

(g) supplies of telecommunication services as defined in Article 24(2);

(h) supplies of game consoles, tablet PC's and laptops;

(i) supplies of cereals and industrial crops including oil seeds and sugar beet, that are not normally used in the unaltered state for final consumption;

(j) supplies of raw and semi-finished metals, including precious metals, where they are not otherwise covered by point (d) of Article 199(1), the special arrangements for second-hand goods, works of art, collector's items and antiques pursuant to Articles 311 to 343 or the special scheme for investment gold pursuant to Articles 344 to 356.

1a. Member States may lay down the conditions for the application of the mechanism provided for in paragraph 1.

1b. The application of the mechanism provided for in paragraph 1 to the supply of any of the goods or services listed in points (c) to (j) of that paragraph is subject to the introduction of appropriate and effective reporting obligations on taxable persons who supply the goods or services to which the mechanism provided for in paragraph 1 applies.

2. Member States shall inform the VAT Committee of the application of the mechanism provided for in paragraph 1 on the introduction of any such mechanism and shall provide the following information to the VAT Committee:

(a) the scope of the measure applying the mechanism together with the type and the features of the fraud, and a detailed description of accompanying measures, including any reporting obligations on taxable persons and any control measures;

(b) actions taken to inform the relevant taxable persons of the introduction of the application of the mechanism;

(c) evaluation criteria to enable comparison between fraudulent activities in relation to the goods and services listed in paragraph 1 before and after the application of the mechanism, fraudulent activities in relation to other goods and services before and after the application of the mechanism, and any increase in other types of fraudulent activities before and after the application of the mechanism;

(d) the date of commencement and the period to be covered by the measure applying the mechanism.

3. Member States applying the mechanism provided for in paragraph 1 shall, on the basis of the evaluation criteria provided for under point (c) of paragraph 2, submit a

report to the Commission no later than 30 June 2017. The report shall clearly indicate the information to be treated as confidential and the information which may be published.

The report shall provide a detailed assessment of the measure's overall effectiveness and efficiency, in particular as regards:

(a) the impact on fraudulent activities in relation to supplies of goods or services covered by the measure;

(b) the possible shift of fraudulent activities to goods or other services;

(c) the compliance costs for taxable persons resulting from the measure.

4. Each Member State that has detected a shift in trends of fraudulent activities in its territory in relation to the goods or services listed in paragraph 1 from the date of entry into force of this Article with respect to such goods or services, shall submit a report to the Commission in that respect no later than 30 June 2017.

Article 199b

1. A Member State may, in cases of imperative urgency and in accordance with paragraphs 2 and 3, designate the recipient as the person liable to pay VAT on specific supplies of goods and services by derogation from Article 193 as a Quick Reaction Mechanism ("QRM") special measure to combat sudden and massive fraud liable to lead to considerable and irreparable financial losses.

The QRM special measure shall be subject to appropriate control measures by the Member State with respect to taxable persons who supply the goods or services to which that measure applies, and shall be for a period not exceeding nine months.

2. A Member State wishing to introduce a QRM special measure as provided for in paragraph 1 shall send a notification to the Commission using the standardized form established in accordance with paragraph 4 and at the same time send it to the other Member States. The Member State shall provide the Commission with the information indicating the sector concerned, the type and the features of the fraud, the existence of imperative grounds of urgency, the sudden and massive character of the fraud and its consequences in terms of considerable and irreparable financial losses. If the Commission considers it does not have all the necessary information, it shall contact the Member State concerned within two weeks of receipt of the notification and specify what additional information is required. Any additional information provided by the Member State concerned to the Commission shall at the same time be sent to the other Member States. If the additional information provided is not sufficient, the Commission shall inform the Member State concerned thereof within one week.

The Member State wishing to introduce a QRM special measure as provided for in paragraph 1 shall at the same time also make an application to the Commission in accordance with the procedure laid down in Article 395(2) and (3).

3. Once the Commission has all the information it considers necessary for appraisal of the notification referred to in the first subparagraph of paragraph 2, it shall notify the Member States thereof. Where it objects to the QRM special measure, it shall produce a negative opinion within one month of that notification, and shall inform the Member State concerned and the VAT Committee thereof. Where the Commission does not object, it shall confirm this in writing to the Member State concerned and to the VAT

Committee within the same time period. The Member State may adopt the QRM special measure from the date of receipt of that confirmation. In appraising the notification, the Commission shall take into account the views of any other Member State sent to it in writing.

4. The Commission shall adopt an implementing act establishing a standardized form for the submission of the notification for the QRM special measure referred to in paragraph 2 and of the information referred to in the first subparagraph of paragraph 2. That implementing act shall be adopted in accordance with the examination procedure referred to in paragraph 5.

5. Where reference is made to this paragraph, Article 5 of Regulation (EU) No 182/2011 of the European Parliament and of the Council shall apply and for this purpose the committee shall be the committee established by Article 58 of Council Regulation (EU) No 904/2010.

Article 200

VAT shall be payable by any person making a taxable intra-Community acquisition of goods.

Article 201

On importation, VAT shall be payable by any person or persons designated or recognized as liable by the Member State of importation.

Article 202

VAT shall be payable by any person who causes goods to cease to be covered by the arrangements or situations listed in Articles 156, 157, 158, 160 and 161.

Article 203

VAT shall be payable by any person who enters the VAT on an invoice.

Article 204

1. Where, pursuant to Articles 193 to 197 and Articles 199 and 200, the person liable for payment of VAT is a taxable person who is not established in the Member State in which the VAT is due, Member States may allow that person to appoint a tax representative as the person liable for payment of the VAT.

Furthermore, where the taxable transaction is carried out by a taxable person who is not established in the Member State in which the VAT is due and no legal instrument exists, with the country in which that taxable person is established or has his seat, relating to mutual assistance similar in scope to that provided for in Directive 76/308/EEC and Regulation (EC) No 1798/2003, Member States may take measures to provide that the person liable for payment of VAT is to be a tax representative appointed by the non-established taxable person.

However, Member States may not apply the option referred to in the second subparagraph to a non-established taxable person, within the meaning of point (1) of Article 358, who has opted for the special scheme for electronically supplied services.

2. The option under the first subparagraph of paragraph 1 shall be subject to the conditions and procedures laid down by each Member State.

Article 205

In the situations referred to in Articles 193 to 200 and Articles 202, 203 and 204, Member States may provide that a person other than the person liable for payment of VAT is to be held jointly and severally liable for payment of VAT.

Section 2: Payment arrangements

Article 206

Any taxable person liable for payment of VAT must pay the net amount of the VAT when submitting the VAT return provided for in Article 250. Member States may, however, set a different date for payment of that amount or may require interim payments to be made.

Article 207

Member States shall take the measures necessary to ensure that persons who are regarded as liable for payment of VAT in the stead of a taxable person not established in their respective territory, in accordance with Articles 194 to 197 and Articles 199 and 204, comply with the payment obligations set out in this Section.

Member States shall also take the measures necessary to ensure that those persons who, in accordance with Article 205, are held to be jointly and severally liable for payment of the VAT comply with these payment obligations.

Article 208

Where Member States designate the customer for investment gold as the person liable for payment of VAT pursuant to Article 198(1) or if, in the case of gold material, semi-manufactured products, or investment gold as defined in Article 344(1), they exercise the option provided for in Article 198(2) of designating the customer as the person liable for payment of VAT, they shall take the measures necessary to ensure that he complies with the payment obligations set out in this Section.

Article 209

Member States shall take the measures necessary to ensure that non-taxable legal persons who are liable for payment of VAT due in respect of intra-Community acquisitions of goods, as referred to in Article 2(1)(b)(i), comply with the payment obligations set out in this Section.

Article 210

Member States shall adopt arrangements for payment of VAT on intra-Community acquisitions of new means of transport, as referred to in Article 2(1)(b)(ii), and on intra-Community acquisitions of products subject to excise duty, as referred to in Article 2(1)(b)(iii).

Article 211

Member States shall lay down the detailed rules for payment in respect of the importation of goods.

In particular, Member States may provide that, in the case of the importation of goods by taxable persons or certain categories thereof, or by persons liable for payment of VAT or certain categories thereof, the VAT due by reason of the importation need not be paid at the time of importation, on condition that it is entered as such in the VAT return to be submitted in accordance with Article 250.

Article 212

Member States may release taxable persons from payment of the VAT due where the amount is insignificant.

Chapter 2 Identification

Article 213

1. Every taxable person shall state when his activity as a taxable person commences, changes or ceases.

Member States shall allow, and may require, the statement to be made by electronic means, in accordance with conditions which they lay down.

2. Without prejudice to the first subparagraph of paragraph 1, every taxable person or non-taxable legal person who makes intra-Community acquisitions of goods which are not subject to VAT pursuant to Article 3(1) must state that he makes such acquisitions if the conditions, laid down in that provision, for not making such transactions subject to VAT cease to be fulfilled.

Article 214

1. Member States shall take the measures necessary to ensure that the following persons are identified by means of an individual number:

    (a) every taxable person, with the exception of those referred to in Article 9(2), who within their respective territory carries out supplies of goods or services in respect of which VAT is deductible, other than supplies of goods or services in respect of which VAT is payable solely by the customer or the person for whom the goods or services are intended, in accordance with Articles 194 to 197 and Article 199;

    (b) every taxable person, or non-taxable legal person, who makes intra-Community acquisitions of goods subject to VAT pursuant to Article 2(1)(b) and every taxable person, or non-taxable legal person, who exercises the option under Article 3(3) of making their intra-Community acquisitions subject to VAT;

    (c) every taxable person who, within their respective territory, makes intra-Community acquisitions of goods for the purposes of transactions which relate to the activities referred to in the second subparagraph of Article 9(1) and which are carried out outside that territory.

    (d) every taxable person who within their respective territory receives services for which he is liable to pay VAT pursuant to Article 196;

    (e) every taxable person, established within their respective territory, who supplies services within the territory of another Member State for which VAT is payable solely by the recipient pursuant to Article 196.

2. Member States need not identify certain taxable persons who carry out transactions on an occasional basis, as referred to in Article 12.

Article 215

Each individual VAT identification number shall have a prefix in accordance with ISO code 3166 — alpha 2 — by which the Member State of issue may be identified.

Nevertheless, Greece may use the prefix "EL".

Article 216

Member States shall take the measures necessary to ensure that their identification systems enable the taxable persons referred to in Article 214 to be identified and to ensure the correct application of the transitional arrangements for the taxation of intra-Community transactions, as referred to in Article 402.

Chapter 3 Invoicing

Section 1: Definition

Article 217

For the purposes of this Directive, "electronic invoice" means an invoice that contains the information required in this Directive, and which has been issued and received in any electronic format.

Section 2: Concept of invoice

Article 218

For the purposes of this Directive, Member States shall accept documents or messages on paper or in electronic form as invoices if they meet the conditions laid down in this Chapter.

Article 219

Any document or message that amends and refers specifically and unambiguously to the initial invoice shall be treated as an invoice.

Section 3: Issue of invoices

Article 219a

Without prejudice to Articles 244 to 248, the following shall apply:

1. Invoicing shall be subject to the rules applying in the Member State in which the supply of goods or services is deemed to be made, in accordance with the provisions of Title V.

2. By way of derogation from point (1), invoicing shall be subject to the rules applying in the Member State in which the supplier has established his business or has a fixed establishment from which the supply is made or, in the absence of such place of establishment or fixed establishment, the Member State where the supplier has his permanent address or usually resides, where:

    (a) the supplier is not established in the Member State in which the supply of goods or services is deemed to be made, in accordance with the provisions of Title V, or his establishment in that Member State does not intervene in the supply within the meaning of Article 192a, and the person liable for the payment of the VAT is the person to whom the goods or services are supplied.

However where the customer issues the invoice (self-billing), point (1) shall apply.

(b) the supply of goods or services is deemed not to be made within the Community, in accordance with the provisions of Title V.

Article 220

1. Every taxable person shall ensure that, in respect of the following, an invoice is issued, either by himself or by his customer or, in his name and on his behalf, by a third party:

    (1) supplies of goods or services which he has made to another taxable person or to a non-taxable legal person;

    (2) supplies of goods as referred to in Article 33;

    (3) supplies of goods carried out in accordance with the conditions specified in Article 138;

    (4) any payment on account made to him before one of the supplies of goods referred to in points (1) and (2) was carried out;

    (5) any payment on account made to him by another taxable person or non-taxable legal person before the provision of services was completed.

2. By way of derogation from paragraph 1, and without prejudice to Article 221(2), the issue of an invoice shall not be required in respect of supplies of services exempted under points (a) to (g) of Article 135(1).

Article 220a

1. Member States shall allow taxable persons to issue a simplified invoice in any of the following cases:

    (a) where the amount of the invoice is not higher than EUR 100 or the equivalent in national currency;

    (b) where the invoice issued is a document or message treated as an invoice pursuant to Article 219.

2. Member States shall not allow taxable persons to issue a simplified invoice where invoices are required to be issued pursuant to points (2) and (3) of Article 220(1) or where the taxable supply of goods or services is carried out by a taxable person who is not established in the Member State in which the VAT is due, or whose establishment in that Member State does not intervene in the supply within the meaning of Article 192a, and the person liable for the payment of VAT is the person to whom the goods or services are supplied.

Article 221

1. Member States may impose on taxable persons an obligation to issue an invoice in accordance with the details required under Article 226 or 226b in respect of supplies of goods or services other than those referred to in Article 220(1).

2. Member States may impose on taxable persons who have established their business in their territory or who have a fixed establishment in their territory from which the supply is made, an obligation to issue an invoice in accordance with the details required in Article 226 or 226b in respect of supplies of services exempted under points (a) to (g) of Article 135(1) which those taxable persons have made in their territory or outside the Community.

3. Member States may release taxable persons from the obligation laid down in Article 220(1) or in Article 220a to issue an invoice in respect of supplies of goods or services which they have made in their territory and which are exempt, with or without deductibility of the VAT paid in the preceding stage, pursuant to Articles 110 and 111, Article 125(1), Article 127, Article 128(1), Article 132, points (h) to (l) of Article 135(1), Articles 136, 371, 375, 376 and 377, Articles 378(2) and 379(2) and Articles 380 to 390c

Article 222

For supplies of goods carried out in accordance with the conditions specified in Article 138 or for supplies of services for which VAT is payable by the customer pursuant to Article 196, an invoice shall be issued no later than on the fifteenth day of the month following that in which the chargeable event occurs.

For other supplies of goods or services Member States may impose time limits on taxable persons for the issue of invoices.

Article 223

Member States shall allow taxable persons to issue summary invoices which detail several separate supplies of goods or services provided that VAT on the supplies mentioned in the summary invoice becomes chargeable during the same calendar month.

Without prejudice to Article 222, Member States may allow summary invoices to include supplies for which VAT has become chargeable during a period of time longer than one calendar month.

Article 224

Invoices may be drawn up by the customer in respect of the supply to him, by a taxable person, of goods or services, where there is a prior agreement between the two parties and provided that a procedure exists for the acceptance of each invoice by the taxable person supplying the goods or services. Member State may require that such invoices be issued in the name and on behalf of the taxable person.

Article 225

Member States may impose specific conditions on taxable persons in cases where the third party, or the customer, who issues invoices is established in a country with which no legal instrument exists relating to mutual assistance similar in scope to that provided for in Directive 2010/24/EU and Regulation (EC) No 1798/2003.

Section 4: Content of invoices

Article 226

Without prejudice to the particular provisions laid down in this Directive, only the following details are required for VAT purposes on invoices issued pursuant to Articles 220 and 221:

(1) the date of issue;

(2) a sequential number, based on one or more series, which uniquely identifies the invoice;

(3) the VAT identification number referred to in Article 214 under which the taxable person supplied the goods or services;

(4) the customer's VAT identification number, as referred to in Article 214, under which the customer received a supply of goods or services in respect of which he is liable for payment of VAT, or received a supply of goods as referred to in Article 138;

(5) the full name and address of the taxable person and of the customer;

(6) the quantity and nature of the goods supplied or the extent and nature of the services rendered;

(7) the date on which the supply of goods or services was made or completed or the date on which the payment on account referred to in points (4) and (5) of Article 220 was made, in so far as that date can be determined and differs from the date of issue of the invoice;

(7a) where the VAT becomes chargeable at the time when the payment is received in accordance with Article 66(b) and the right of deduction arises at the time the deductible tax becomes chargeable, the mention "Cash accounting";

(8) the taxable amount per rate or exemption, the unit price exclusive of VAT and any discounts or rebates if they are not included in the unit price;

(9) the VAT rate applied;

(10) the VAT amount payable, except where a special arrangement is applied under which, in accordance with this Directive, such a detail is excluded;

(10a) where the customer receiving a supply issues the invoice instead of the supplier, the mention "Self-billing";

(11) in the case of an exemption, reference to the applicable provision of this Directive, or to the corresponding national provision, or any other reference indicating that the supply of goods or services is exempt;

(11a) where the customer is liable for the payment of the VAT, the mention "Reverse charge";

(12) in the case of the supply of a new means of transport made in accordance with the conditions specified in Article 138(1) and (2)(a), the characteristics as identified in point (b) of Article 2(2);

(13) where the margin scheme for travel agents is applied, the mention "Margin scheme — Travel agents";

(14) where one of the special arrangements applicable to second-hand goods, works of art, collectors' items and antiques is applied, the mention "Margin scheme — Second-hand goods"; "Margin scheme — Works of art" or "Margin scheme — Collector's items and antiques" respectively";

(15) where the person liable for payment of VAT is a tax representative for the purposes of Article 204, the VAT identification number, referred to in Article 214, of that tax representative, together with his full name and address.

Article 226a

Where the invoice is issued by a taxable person, who is not established in the Member State where the tax is due or whose establishment in that Member State does not intervene in the supply within the meaning of Article 192a, and who is making a supply of goods or services to a customer who is liable for payment of VAT, the taxable person may omit the details referred to in points (8), (9) and (10) of Article 226 and instead indicate, by reference to the quantity or extent of the goods or services supplied and their nature, the taxable amount of those goods or services.

Article 226b

As regards simplified invoices issued pursuant to Article 220a and Article 221(1) and (2), Member States shall require at least the following details:

- (a) the date of issue;
- (b) identification of the taxable person supplying the goods or services;
- (c) identification of the type of goods or services supplied;
- (d) the VAT amount payable or the information needed to calculate it;
- (e) where the invoice issued is a document or message treated as an invoice pursuant to Article 219, specific and unambiguous reference to that initial invoice and the specific details which are being amended.

They may not require details on invoices other than those referred to in Articles 226, 227 and 230.

Article 227

Member States may require taxable persons established in their territory and supplying goods or services there to indicate the VAT identification number, referred to in Article 214, of the customer in cases other than those referred to in point (4) of Article 226.

Article 228

[Deleted]

Article 229

Member States shall not require invoices to be signed.

Article 230

The amounts which appear on the invoice may be expressed in any currency, provided that the amount of VAT payable or to be adjusted is expressed in the national currency of the Member State, using the conversion rate mechanism provided for in Article 91.

Article 231

[Deleted]

Section 5: Paper invoices and electronic invoices

Article 232

The use of an electronic invoice shall be subject to acceptance by the recipient.

Article 233

1. The authenticity of the origin, the integrity of the content and the legibility of an invoice, whether on paper or in electronic form, shall be ensured from the point in time of issue until the end of the period for storage of the invoice.

   Each taxable person shall determine the way to ensure the authenticity of the origin, the integrity of the content and the legibility of the invoice. This may be achieved by any business controls which create a reliable audit trail between an invoice and a supply of goods or services.

   "Authenticity of the origin" means the assurance of the identity of the supplier or the issuer of the invoice.

   "Integrity of the content" means that the content required according to this Directive has not been altered.

2. Other than by way of the type of business controls described in paragraph 1, the following are examples of technologies that ensure the authenticity of the origin and the integrity of the content of an electronic invoice:

   (a) an advanced electronic signature within the meaning of point (2) of Article 2 of Directive 1999/93/EC of the European Parliament and of the Council of 13 December 1999 on a Community framework for electronic signatures, based on a qualified certificate and created by a secure signature creation device, within the meaning of points (6) and (10) of Article 2 of Directive 1999/93/EC;

   (b) electronic data interchange (EDI), as defined in Article 2 of Annex 1 to Commission Recommendation 1994/820/EC of 19 October 1994 relating to the legal aspects of electronic data interchange, where the agreement relating to the exchange provides for the use of procedures guaranteeing the authenticity of the origin and integrity of the data.

Article 234

[Deleted]

Article 235

Member States may lay down specific conditions for electronic invoices issued in respect of goods or services supplied in their territory from a country with which no legal instrument exists relating to mutual assistance similar in scope to that provided for in Directive

2010/24/EU and Regulation (EC) No 1798/2003.

Article 236

Where batches containing several electronic invoices are sent or made available to the same recipient, the details common to the individual invoices may be mentioned only once where, for each invoice, all the information is accessible.

Article 237

By 31 December 2016 at the latest, the Commission shall present to the European Parliament and the Council an overall assessment report, based on an independent economic study, on the impact of the invoicing rules applicable from 1 January 2013 and notably on the extent to which they have effectively led to a decrease in administrative burdens for businesses, accompanied where necessary by an appropriate proposal to amend the relevant rules.

Section 6: Simplification measures

Article 238

1. After consulting the VAT Committee, Member States may, in accordance with conditions which they may lay down, provide that in the following cases only the information required pursuant to Article 226b shall be entered on invoices in respect of supplies of goods or services:

    (a) where the amount of the invoice is higher than EUR 100 but not higher than EUR 400, or the equivalent in national currency;

    (b) where commercial or administrative practice in the business sector concerned or the technical conditions under which the invoices are issued make it particularly difficult to comply with all the obligations referred to in Article 226 or 230.

2. [Deleted]

3. The simplified arrangements provided for in paragraph 1 shall not be applied where invoices are required to be issued pursuant to points (2) and (3) of Article 220(1) or where the taxable supply of goods or services is carried out by a taxable person who is not established in the Member State in which the VAT is due or whose establishment in that Member State does not intervene in the supply within the meaning of Article 192a and the person liable for the payment of VAT is the person to whom the goods or services are supplied.

Article 239

In cases where Member States make use of the option under point (b) of the first subparagraph of Article 272(1) of not allocating a VAT identification number to taxable persons who do not carry out any of the transactions referred to in Articles 20, 21, 22, 33, 36, 138 and 141, and where the supplier or the customer has not been allocated an identification number of that type, another number called the tax reference number, as defined by the Member States concerned, shall be entered on the invoice instead.

Article 240

Where the taxable person has been allocated a VAT identification number, the Member States exercising the option under point (b) of the first subparagraph of Article 272(1) may also require the invoice to show the following:

    (1) in respect of the supply of services, as referred to in Articles 44, 47, 50, 53, 54 and 55, and the supply of goods, as referred to in Articles 138 and 141, the VAT identification number and the tax reference number of the supplier;

    (2) in respect of other supplies of goods or services, only the tax reference number of the supplier or only the VAT identification number.

RECAST VAT DIRECTIVE

Chapter 4 Accounting

Section 1: Definition

Article 241

For the purposes of this Chapter, "storage of an invoice by electronic means" shall mean storage of data using electronic equipment for processing (including digital compression) and storage, and employing wire, radio, optical or other electromagnetic means.

Section 2: General obligations

Article 242

Every taxable person shall keep accounts in sufficient detail for VAT to be applied and its application checked by the tax authorities.

Article 243

1. Every taxable person shall keep a register of the goods dispatched or transported by him, or on his behalf, to a destination outside the territory of the Member State of departure but within the Community for the purposes of transactions consisting in valuations of those goods or work on them or their temporary use as referred to in points (f), (g) and (h) of Article 17(2).

2. Every taxable person shall keep accounts in sufficient detail to enable the identification of goods dispatched to him from another Member State, by or on behalf of a taxable person identified for VAT purposes in that other Member State, and used for services consisting in valuations of those goods or work on those goods.

Section 3: Specific obligations relating to the storage of all invoices

Article 244

Every taxable person shall ensure that copies of the invoices issued by himself, or by his customer or, in his name and on his behalf, by a third party, and all the invoices which he has received, are stored.

Article 245

1. For the purposes of this Directive, the taxable person may decide the place of storage of all invoices provided that he makes the invoices or information stored in accordance

with Article 244 available to the competent authorities without undue delay whenever they so request.

2. Member States may require taxable persons established in their territory to notify them of the place of storage, if it is outside their territory.

Member States may also require taxable persons established in their territory to store within that territory invoices issued by themselves or by their customers or, in their name and on their behalf, by a third party, as well as all the invoices that they have received, when the storage is not by electronic means guaranteeing full on-line access to the data concerned.

Article 246

[Deleted]

Article 247

1. Each Member State shall determine the period throughout which taxable persons must ensure the storage of invoices relating to the supply of goods or services in its territory and invoices received by taxable persons established in its territory.

2. In order to ensure that the requirements laid down in Article 233 are met, the Member State referred to in paragraph 1 may require that invoices be stored in the original form in which they were sent or made available, whether paper or electronic. Additionally, in the case of invoices stored by electronic means, the Member State may require that the data guaranteeing the authenticity of the origin of the invoices and the integrity of their content, as provided for in Article 233, also be stored by electronic means.

3. The Member State referred to in paragraph 1 may lay down specific conditions prohibiting or restricting the storage of invoices in a country with which no legal instrument exists relating to mutual assistance similar in scope to that provided for in Directive 2010/24/EU and Regulation (EC) No 1798/2003 or to the right referred to in Article 249 to access by electronic means, to download and to use.

Article 248

Member States may, subject to conditions which they lay down, require the storage of invoices received by non-taxable persons.

Article 248a

For control purposes, and as regards invoices in respect of supplies of goods or services supplied in their territory and invoices received by taxable persons established in their territory, Member States may, for certain taxable persons or certain cases, require translation into their official languages. Member States may, however, not impose a general requirement that invoices be translated.

Section 4: Right of access to invoices stored by electronic means in another Member State

Article 249

For control purposes, where a taxable person stores, by electronic means guaranteeing online access to the data concerned, invoices which he issues or receives, the competent authorities of the Member State in which he is established and, where the VAT is due in another Member State, the competent authorities of that Member State, shall have the right to access, download and use those invoices.

Chapter 5 Returns

Article 250

1. Every taxable person shall submit a VAT return setting out all the information needed to calculate the tax that has become chargeable and the deductions to be made including, in so far as is necessary for the establishment of the basis of assessment, the total value of the transactions relating to such tax and deductions and the value of any exempt transactions.

2. Member States shall allow, and may require, the VAT return referred to in paragraph 1 to be submitted by electronic means, in accordance with conditions which they lay down.

Article 251

In addition to the information referred to in Article 250, the VAT return covering a given tax period shall show the following:

   (a) the total value, exclusive of VAT, of the supplies of goods referred to in Article 138 in respect of which VAT has become chargeable during this tax period;

   (b) the total value, exclusive of VAT, of the supplies of goods referred to in Articles 33 and 36 carried out within the territory of another Member State, in respect of which VAT has become chargeable during this tax period, where the place where dispatch or transport of the goods began is situated in the Member State in which the return must be submitted;

   (c) the total value, exclusive of VAT, of the intra-Community acquisitions of goods, or transactions treated as such, pursuant to Articles 21 or 22, made in the Member State in which the return must be submitted and in respect of which VAT has become chargeable during this tax period;

   (d) the total value, exclusive of VAT, of the supplies of goods referred to in Articles 33 and 36 carried out in the Member State in which the return must be submitted and in respect of which VAT has become chargeable during this tax period, where the place where dispatch or transport of the goods began is situated within the territory of another Member State;

   (e) the total value, exclusive of VAT, of the supplies of goods carried out in the Member State in which the return must be submitted and in respect of which the taxable person has been designated, in accordance with Article 197, as liable for payment of VAT and in respect of which VAT has become chargeable during this tax period.

Article 252

1. The VAT return shall be submitted by a deadline to be determined by Member States. That deadline may not be more than two months after the end of each tax period.

2. The tax period shall be set by each Member State at one month, two months or three months.

Member States may, however, set different tax periods provided that those periods do not exceed one year.

Article 253

Sweden may apply a simplified procedure for small and medium-sized enterprises, whereby taxable persons carrying out only transactions taxable at national level may submit VAT returns three months after the end of the annual direct tax period.

Article 254

In the case of supplies of new means of transport carried out in accordance with the conditions specified in Article 138(2)(a) by a taxable person identified for VAT purposes for a customer not identified for VAT purposes, or by a taxable person as defined in Article 9(2), Member States shall take the measures necessary to ensure that the vendor communicates all the information needed for VAT to be applied and its application checked by the tax authorities.

Article 255

Where Member States designate the customer of investment gold as the person liable for payment of VAT pursuant to Article 198(1) or if, in the case of gold material, semi-manufactured products or investment gold as defined in Article 344(1), they exercise the option provided for in Article 198(2) of designating the customer as the person liable for payment of VAT, they shall take the measures necessary to ensure that he complies with the obligations relating to submission of a VAT return set out in this Chapter.

Article 256

Member States shall take the measures necessary to ensure that persons who are regarded as liable for payment of VAT in the stead of a taxable person not established within their territory, in accordance with Articles 194 to 197 and Article 204, comply with the obligations relating to submission of a VAT return, as laid down in this Chapter.

Article 257

Member States shall take the measures necessary to ensure that non-taxable legal persons who are liable for payment of VAT due in respect of intra-Community acquisitions of goods, as referred to in Article 2(1)(b)(i), comply with the obligations relating to submission of a VAT return, as laid down in this Chapter.

Article 258

Member States shall lay down detailed rules for the submission of VAT returns in respect of intra-Community acquisitions of new means of transport, as referred to in Article 2(1)(b)(ii), and intra-Community acquisitions of products subject to excise duty, as referred to in Article

2(1)(b)(iii).

Article 259

Member States may require persons who make intra-Community acquisitions of new means of transport as referred to in Article 2(1)(b)(ii), to provide, when submitting the VAT return, all the information needed for VAT to be applied and its application checked by the tax authorities.

Article 260

Member States shall lay down detailed rules for the submission of VAT returns in respect of the importation of goods.

Article 261

1. Member States may require the taxable person to submit a return showing all the particulars specified in Articles 250 and 251 in respect of all transactions carried out in the preceding year. That return shall provide all the information necessary for any adjustments.

2. Member States shall allow, and may require, the return referred to in paragraph 1 to be submitted by electronic means, in accordance with conditions which they lay down.

Chapter 6 Recapitulative Statements

Article 262

Every taxable person identified for VAT purposes shall submit a recapitulative statement of the following:

(a) the acquirers identified for VAT purposes to whom he has supplied goods in accordance with the conditions specified in Article 138(1) and (2)(c);

(b) the persons identified for VAT purposes to whom he has supplied goods which were supplied to him by way of intra-Community acquisitions referred to in Article 42;

(c) the taxable persons, and the non-taxable legal persons identified for VAT purposes, to whom he has supplied services, other than services that are exempted from VAT in the Member State where the transaction is taxable, and for which the recipient is liable to pay the tax pursuant to Article 196.

Article 263

1. The recapitulative statement shall be drawn up for each calendar month within a period not exceeding one month and in accordance with procedures to be determined by the Member States.

1a. However, Member States, in accordance with the conditions and limits which they may lay down, may allow taxable persons to submit the recapitulative statement for each calendar quarter within a time limit not exceeding one month from the end of the quarter, where the total quarterly amount, excluding VAT, of the supplies of goods as referred to in Articles 264(1)(d) and 265(1)(c) does not exceed either in respect of the quarter concerned or in respect of any of the previous four quarters the sum of EUR 50 000 or its equivalent in national currency.

The option provided for in the first subparagraph shall cease to be applicable after the end of the month during which the total value, excluding VAT, of the supplies of goods as referred to in Article 264(1)(d) and 265(1)(c) exceeds, in respect of the current quarter, the sum of EUR 50 000 or its equivalent in national currency. In this case, a recapitulative statement shall be drawn up for the month(s) which has (have) elapsed since the beginning of the quarter, within a time limit not exceeding one month.

1b. Until 31 December 2011, Member States are allowed to set the sum mentioned in paragraph 1a at EUR 100 000 or its equivalent in national currency.

1c. In the case of supplies of services as referred to in Article 264(1)(d), Member States, in accordance with the conditions and limits which they may lay down, may allow taxable persons to submit the recapitulative statement for each calendar quarter within a time limit not exceeding one month from the end of the quarter.

Member States may, in particular, require the taxable persons who carry out supplies of both goods and services as referred to in Article 264(1)(d) to submit the recapitulative statement in accordance with the deadline resulting from paragraphs 1 to 1b.

2. Member States shall allow, and may require, the recapitulative statement referred to in paragraph 1 to be submitted by electronic file transfer, in accordance with conditions which they lay down.

Article 264

1. The recapitulative statement shall set out the following information:

    (a) the VAT identification number of the taxable person in the Member State in which the recapitulative statement must be submitted and under which he has carried out the supply of goods in accordance with the conditions specified in Article 138(1) and under which he effected taxable supplies of services in accordance with the conditions laid down in Article 44;

    (b) the VAT identification number of the person acquiring the goods or receiving the services in a Member State other than that in which the recapitulative statement must be submitted and under which the goods or services were supplied to him;

    (c) the VAT identification number of the taxable person in the Member State in which the recapitulative statement must be submitted and under which he has carried out a transfer to another Member State, as referred to in Article 138(2)(c), and the number by means of which he is identified in the Member State in which the dispatch or transport ended;

    (d) for each person who acquired goods or received services, the total value of the supplies of goods and the total value of the supplies of services carried out by the taxable person;

    (e) in respect of supplies of goods consisting in transfers to another Member State, as referred to in Article 138(2)(c), the total value of the supplies, determined in accordance with Article 76;

    (f) the amounts of adjustments made pursuant to Article 90.

2. The value referred to in paragraph 1(d) shall be declared for the period of submission established in accordance with Article 263(1) to (1c) during which VAT became chargeable.

The amounts referred to in paragraph 1(f) shall be declared for the period of submission established in accordance with Article 263(1) to (1c) during which the person acquiring the goods was notified of the adjustment.

Article 265

1. In the case of intra-Community acquisitions of goods, as referred to in Article 42, the taxable person identified for VAT purposes in the Member State which issued him with the VAT identification number under which he made such acquisitions shall set the following information out clearly on the recapitulative statement:

    (a) his VAT identification number in that Member State and under which he made the acquisition and subsequent supply of goods;

(b) the VAT identification number, in the Member State in which dispatch or transport of the goods ended, of the person to whom the subsequent supply was made by the taxable person;

(c) for each person to whom the subsequent supply was made, the total value, exclusive of VAT, of the supplies made by the taxable person in the Member State in which dispatch or transport of the goods ended.

2. The value referred to in paragraph 1(c) shall be declared for the period of submission established in accordance with Article 263(1) to (1b) during which VAT became chargeable.

Article 266

By way of derogation from Articles 264 and 265, Member States may provide that additional information is to be given in recapitulative statements.

Article 267

Member States shall take the measures necessary to ensure that those persons who, in accordance with Articles 194 and 204, are regarded as liable for payment of VAT, in the stead of a taxable person who is not established in their territory, comply with the obligation to submit a recapitulative statement as provided for in this Chapter.

Article 268

Member States may require that taxable persons who, in their territory, make intra-Community acquisitions of goods, or transactions treated as such, pursuant to Articles 21 or 22, submit statements giving details of such acquisitions, provided, however, that such statements are not required in respect of a period of less than one month.

Article 269

Acting unanimously on a proposal from the Commission, the Council may authorize any Member State to introduce the special measures provided for in Articles 270 and 271 to simplify the obligation, laid down in this Chapter, to submit a recapitulative statement. Such measures may not jeopardize the proper monitoring of intra-Community transactions.

Article 270

By virtue of the authorization referred to in Article 269, Member States may permit taxable persons to submit annual recapitulative statements indicating the VAT identification numbers, in another Member State, of the persons to whom those taxable persons have supplied goods in accordance with the conditions specified in Article 138(1) and (2)(c), where the taxable persons meet the following three conditions:

(a) the total annual value, exclusive of VAT, of their supplies of goods and services does not exceed by more than EUR 35,000, or the equivalent in national currency, the amount of the annual turnover which is used as a reference for application of the exemption for small enterprises provided for in Articles 282 to 292;

(b) the total annual value, exclusive of VAT, of supplies of goods carried out by them in accordance with the conditions specified in Article 138 does not exceed EUR 15,000 or the equivalent in national currency;

(c) none of the supplies of goods carried out by them in accordance with the conditions specified in Article 138 is a supply of new means of transport.

Article 271

By virtue of the authorization referred to in Article 269, Member States which set at over three months the tax period in respect of which taxable persons must submit the VAT return provided for in Article 250 may permit such persons to submit recapitulative statements in respect of the same period where those taxable persons meet the following three conditions:

(a) the total annual value, exclusive of VAT, of their supplies of goods and services does not exceed EUR 200,000 or the equivalent in national currency;

(b) the total annual value, exclusive of VAT, of supplies of goods carried out by them in accordance with the conditions specified in Article 138 does not exceed EUR 15,000 or the equivalent in national currency;

(c) none of the supplies of goods carried out by them in accordance with the conditions specified in Article 138 is a supply of new means of transport.

Chapter 7 Miscellaneous Provisions

Article 272

1. Member States may release the following taxable persons from certain or all obligations referred to in Chapters 2 to 6:

    (a) taxable persons whose intra-Community acquisitions of goods are not subject to VAT pursuant to Article 3(1);

    (b) taxable persons carrying out none of the transactions referred to in Articles 20, 21, 22, 33, 36, 138 and 141;

    (c) taxable persons carrying out only supplies of goods or of services which are exempt pursuant to Articles 132, 135 and 136, Articles 146 to 149 and Articles 151, 152 or 153;

    (d) taxable persons covered by the exemption for small enterprises provided for in Articles 282 to 292;

    (e) taxable persons covered by the common flat-rate scheme for farmers.

    Member States may not release the taxable persons referred to in point (b) of the first subparagraph from the invoicing obligations laid down in Sections 3 to 6 of Chapter 3 and Section 3 of Chapter 4.

2. If Member States exercise the option under point (e) of the first subparagraph of paragraph 1, they shall take the measures necessary to ensure the correct application of the transitional arrangements for the taxation of intra-Community transactions.

3. Member States may release taxable persons other than those referred to in paragraph 1 from certain of the accounting obligations referred to in Article 242.

Article 273

Member States may impose other obligations which they deem necessary to ensure the correct collection of VAT and to prevent evasion, subject to the requirement of equal treatment as between domestic transactions and transactions carried out between Member States by taxable persons and provided that such obligations do not, in trade between Member States, give rise to formalities connected with the crossing of frontiers.

The option under the first paragraph may not be relied upon in order to impose additional invoicing obligations over and above those laid down in Chapter 3.

Chapter 8 Obligations Relating to Certain Importations and Exportations

Section 1: Importation

Article 274

Articles 275, 276 and 277 shall apply to the importation of goods in free circulation which enter the Community from a third territory forming part of the customs territory of the Community.

Article 275

The formalities relating to the importation of the goods referred to in Article 274 shall be the same as those laid down by the Community customs provisions in force for the importation of goods into the customs territory of the Community.

Article 276

Where dispatch or transport of the goods referred to in Article 274 ends at a place situated outside the Member State of their entry into the Community, they shall circulate in the Community under the internal Community transit procedure laid down by the Community customs provisions in force, in so far as they have been the subject of a declaration placing them under that procedure on their entry into the Community.

Article 277

Where, on their entry into the Community, the goods referred to in Article 274 are in one of the situations which would entitle them, if they were imported within the meaning of the first paragraph of Article 30, to be covered by one of the arrangements or situations referred to in Article 156, or by a temporary importation arrangement with full exemption from import duties, Member States shall take the measures necessary to ensure that the goods may remain in the Community under the same conditions as those laid down for the application of those arrangements or situations.

Section 2: Exportation

Article 278

Articles 279 and 280 shall apply to the exportation of goods in free circulation which are dispatched or transported from a Member State to a third territory forming part of the customs territory of the Community.

Article 279

The formalities relating to the exportation of the goods referred to in Article 278 from the territory of the Community shall be the same as those laid down by the Community customs provisions in force for the exportation of goods from the customs territory of the Community.

Article 280

In the case of goods which are temporarily exported from the Community, in order to be reimported, Member States shall take the measures necessary to ensure that, on reimportation into the Community, such goods may be covered by the same provisions as would have applied if they had been temporarily exported from the customs territory of the Community.

Title XII - Special Schemes

Chapter 1 Special Scheme for Small Enterprises

Section 1: Simplified procedures for charging and collection

Article 281

Member States which might encounter difficulties in applying the normal VAT arrangements to small enterprises, by reason of the activities or structure of such enterprises, may, subject to such conditions and limits as they may set, and after consulting the VAT Committee, apply simplified procedures, such as flat-rate schemes, for charging and collecting VAT provided that they do not lead to a reduction thereof.

Section 2: Exemptions or graduated relief

Article 282

The exemptions and graduated tax relief provided for in this Section shall apply to the supply of goods and services by small enterprises.

Article 283

1. The arrangements provided for in this Section shall not apply to the following transactions:

    (a) transactions carried out on an occasional basis, as referred to in Article 12;

    (b) supplies of new means of transport carried out in accordance with the conditions specified in Article 138(1) and (2)(a);

    (c) supplies of goods or services carried out by a taxable person who is not established in the Member State in which the VAT is due.

2. Member States may exclude transactions other than those referred to in paragraph 1 from the arrangements provided for in this Section.

Article 284

1. Member States which have exercised the option under Article 14 of Council Directive 67/228/EEC of 11 April 1967 on the harmonization of legislation of Member States concerning turnover taxes — Structure and procedures for application of the common system of value added tax of introducing exemptions or graduated tax relief may retain them, and the arrangements for applying them, if they comply with the VAT rules.

2. Member States which, at 17 May 1977, exempted taxable persons whose annual turnover was less than the equivalent in national currency of 5000 European units of account at the conversion rate on that date, may raise that ceiling up to EUR 5000.

Member States which applied graduated tax relief may neither raise the ceiling for graduated tax relief nor render the conditions for the granting of it more favorable.

Article 285

Member States which have not exercised the option under Article 14 of Directive 67/228/EEC may exempt taxable persons whose annual turnover is no higher than EUR 5000 or the equivalent in national currency.

The Member States referred to in the first paragraph may grant graduated tax relief to taxable persons whose annual turnover exceeds the ceiling fixed by them for its application.

Article 286

Member States which, at 17 May 1977, exempted taxable persons whose annual turnover was equal to or higher than the equivalent in national currency of 5000 European units of account at the conversion rate on that date, may raise that ceiling in order to maintain the value of the exemption in real terms.

Article 287

Member States which acceded after 1 January 1978 may exempt taxable persons whose annual turnover is no higher than the equivalent in national currency of the following amounts at the conversion rate on the day of their accession:

(1) Greece: 10,000 European units of account;

(2) Spain: ECU 10,000;

(3) Portugal: ECU 10,000;

(4) Austria: ECU 35,000;

(5) Finland: ECU 10,000;

(6) Sweden: ECU 10,000;

(7) Czech Republic: EUR 35,000;

(8) Estonia: EUR 16,000;

(9) Cyprus: EUR 15,600;

(10) Latvia: EUR 17,200;

(11) Lithuania: EUR 29,000;

(12) Hungary: EUR 35,000;

(13) Malta: EUR 37,000 if the economic activity consists principally in the supply of goods, EUR 24,300 if the economic activity consists principally in the supply of services with a low value added (high inputs), and EUR 14,600 in other cases, namely supplies of services with a high value added (low inputs);

(14) Poland: EUR 10,000;

(15) Slovenia: EUR 25,000;

(16) Slovakia: EUR 35,000.

(17) Bulgaria: EUR 25,600;

(18) Romania: EUR 35,000.

(19) Croatia: EUR 35,000.

Article 288

The turnover serving as a reference for the purposes of applying the arrangements provided for in this Section shall consist of the following amounts, exclusive of VAT:

(1) the value of supplies of goods and services, in so far as they are taxed;

(2) the value of transactions which are exempt, with deductibility of the VAT paid at the preceding stage, pursuant to Articles 110 or 111, Article 125(1), Article 127 or Article 128(1);

(3) the value of transactions which are exempt pursuant to Articles 146 to 149 and Articles 151, 152 or 153;

(4) the value of real estate transactions, financial transactions as referred to in points (b) to (g) of Article 135(1), and insurance services, unless those transactions are ancillary transactions.

However, disposals of the tangible or intangible capital assets of an enterprise shall not be taken into account for the purposes of calculating turnover.

Article 289

Taxable persons exempt from VAT shall not be entitled to deduct VAT in accordance with Articles 167 to 171 and Articles 173 to 177, and may not show the VAT on their invoices.

Article 290

Taxable persons who are entitled to exemption from VAT may opt either for the normal VAT arrangements or for the simplified procedures provided for in Article 281. In this case, they shall be entitled to any graduated tax relief provided for under national legislation.

Article 291

Subject to the application of Article 281, taxable persons enjoying graduated relief shall be regarded as taxable persons subject to the normal VAT arrangements.

Article 292

The arrangements provided for in this Section shall apply until a date to be fixed by the Council in accordance with Article 93 of the Treaty, which may not be later than that on which the definitive arrangements referred to in Article 402 enter into force.

Section 3: Reporting and review

Article 293

Every four years starting from the adoption of this Directive, the Commission shall present to the Council, on the basis of information obtained from the Member States, a report on the application of this Chapter, together, where appropriate and taking into account the need to ensure the long-term convergence of national regulations, with proposals on the following subjects:

    (1) improvements to the special scheme for small enterprises;

    (2) the adaptation of national systems as regards exemptions and graduated tax relief;

    (3) the adaptation of the ceilings provided for in Section 2.

Article 294

The Council shall decide, in accordance with Article 93 of the Treaty, whether a special scheme for small enterprises is necessary under the definitive arrangements and, if appropriate, shall lay down the common limits and conditions for the implementation of that scheme.

Chapter 2 Common Flat-Rate Scheme for Farmers

Article 295

1. For the purposes of this Chapter, the following definitions shall apply:

    (1) "farmer" means any taxable person whose activity is carried out in an agricultural, forestry or fisheries undertaking;

    (2) "agricultural, forestry or fisheries undertaking" means an undertaking regarded as such by each Member State within the framework of the production activities listed in Annex VII;

    (3) "flat-rate farmer" means any farmer covered by the flat-rate scheme provided for in this Chapter;

    (4) "agricultural products" means goods produced by an agricultural, forestry or fisheries undertaking in each Member State as a result of the activities listed in Annex VII;

    (5) "agricultural services" means services, and in particular those listed in Annex VIII, supplied by a farmer using his labor force or the equipment normally employed in the agricultural, forestry or fisheries undertaking operated by him and normally playing a part in agricultural production;

    (6) "input VAT charged" means the amount of the total VAT attaching to the goods and services purchased by all agricultural, forestry and fisheries undertakings of each Member State subject to the flat-rate scheme where such tax would be deductible in accordance with Articles 167, 168 and 169 and Articles 173 to 177 by a farmer subject to the normal VAT arrangements;

    (7) "flat-rate compensation percentages" means the percentages fixed by Member States in accordance with Articles 297, 298 and 299 and applied by them in the cases specified in Article 300 in order to enable flat-rate farmers to offset at a fixed rate the input VAT charged;

    (8) "flat-rate compensation" means the amount arrived at by applying the flat-rate compensation percentage to the turnover of the flat-rate farmer in the cases specified in Article 300.

2. Where a farmer processes, using means normally employed in an agricultural, forestry or fisheries undertaking, products deriving essentially from his agricultural production, such processing activities shall be treated as agricultural production activities, as listed in Annex VII.

Article 296

1. Where the application to farmers of the normal VAT arrangements, or the special scheme provided for in Chapter 1, is likely to give rise to difficulties, Member States may apply to farmers, in accordance with this Chapter, a flat-rate scheme designed to offset the VAT charged on purchases of goods and services made by the flat-rate farmers.

2. Each Member State may exclude from the flat-rate scheme certain categories of farmers, as well as farmers for whom application of the normal VAT arrangements, or of the simplified procedures provided for in Article 281, is not likely to give rise to administrative difficulties.

3. Every flat-rate farmer may opt, subject to the rules and conditions to be laid down by each Member State, for application of the normal VAT arrangements or, as the case may be, the simplified procedures provided for in Article 281.

Article 297

Member States shall, where necessary, fix the flat-rate compensation percentages. They may fix varying percentages for forestry, for the different sub-divisions of agriculture and for fisheries.

Member States shall notify the Commission of the flat-rate compensation percentages fixed in accordance with the first paragraph before applying them.

Article 298

The flat-rate compensation percentages shall be calculated on the basis of macro-economic statistics for flat-rate farmers alone for the preceding three years.

The percentages may be rounded up or down to the nearest half-point. Member States may also reduce such percentages to a nil rate.

Article 299

The flat-rate compensation percentages may not have the effect of obtaining for flat-rate farmers refunds greater than the input VAT charged.

Article 300

The flat-rate compensation percentages shall be applied to the prices, exclusive of VAT, of the following goods and services:

(1) agricultural products supplied by flat-rate farmers to taxable persons other than those covered, in the Member State in which these products were supplied, by this flat-rate scheme;

(2) agricultural products supplied by flat-rate farmers, in accordance with the conditions specified in Article 138, to non-taxable legal persons whose intra-Community acquisitions of goods are subject to VAT, pursuant to Article 2(1)(b), in the Member State in which dispatch or transport of those agricultural products ends;

(3) agricultural services supplied by flat-rate farmers to taxable persons other than those covered, in the Member State in which these services were supplied, by this flat-rate scheme.

Article 301

1. In the case of the supply of agricultural products or agricultural services specified in Article 300, Member States shall provide that the flat-rate compensation is to be paid either by the customer or by the public authorities.

2. In respect of any supply of agricultural products or agricultural services other than those specified in Article 300, the flat-rate compensation shall be deemed to be paid by the customer.

Article 302

If a flat-rate farmer is entitled to flat-rate compensation, he shall not be entitled to deduction of VAT in respect of activities covered by this flat-rate scheme.

Article 303

1. Where the taxable customer pays flat-rate compensation pursuant to Article 301(1), he shall be entitled, in accordance with the conditions laid down in Articles 167, 168 and 169 and Articles 173 to 177 and the procedures laid down by the Member States, to deduct the compensation amount from the VAT for which he is liable in the Member State in which his taxed transactions are carried out.

2. Member States shall refund to the customer the amount of the flat-rate compensation he has paid in respect of any of the following transactions:

    (a) the supply of agricultural products, carried out in accordance with the conditions specified in Article 138, to taxable persons, or to non-taxable legal persons, acting as such in another Member State within the territory of which their intra-Community acquisitions of goods are subject to VAT pursuant to Article 2(1)(b);

    (b) the supply of agricultural products, carried out in accordance with the conditions specified in Articles 146, 147, 148 and 156, Article 157(1)(b) and Articles 158, 160 and 161, to a taxable customer established outside the Community, in so far as the products are used by that customer for the purposes of the transactions referred to in Article 169(a) and (b) or for the purposes of supplies of services which are deemed to take place within the territory of the Member State in which the customer is established and in respect of which VAT is payable solely by the customer pursuant to Article 196;

    (c) the supply of agricultural services to a taxable customer established within the Community but in another Member State or to a taxable customer established outside the Community, in so far as the services are used by the customer for the purposes of the transactions referred to in Article 169(a) and (b) or for the purposes of supplies of services which are deemed to take place within the territory of the Member State in which the customer is established and in respect of which VAT is payable solely by the customer pursuant to Article 196.

3. Member States shall determine the method by which the refunds provided for in paragraph 2 are to be made. In particular, they may apply the provisions of Directives 79/1072/EEC and 86/560/EEC.

Article 304

Member States shall take all measures necessary to verify payments of flat-rate compensation to flat-rate farmers.

Article 305

Whenever Member States apply this flat-rate scheme, they shall take all measures necessary to ensure that the supply of agricultural products between Member States, carried out in accordance with the conditions specified in Article 33, is always taxed in the same way, whether the supply is effected by a flat-rate farmer or by another taxable person.

Chapter 3 Special Scheme for Travel Agents

Article 306

1. Member States shall apply a special VAT scheme, in accordance with this Chapter, to transactions carried out by travel agents who deal with customers in their own name and use supplies of goods or services provided by other taxable persons, in the provision of travel facilities.

This special scheme shall not apply to travel agents where they act solely as intermediaries and to whom point (c) of the first paragraph of Article 79 applies for the purposes of calculating the taxable amount.

2. For the purposes of this Chapter, tour operators shall be regarded as travel agents.

Article 307

Transactions made, in accordance with the conditions laid down in Article 306, by the travel agent in respect of a journey shall be regarded as a single service supplied by the travel agent to the traveler.

The single service shall be taxable in the Member State in which the travel agent has established his business or has a fixed establishment from which the travel agent has carried out the supply of services.

Article 308

The taxable amount and the price exclusive of VAT, within the meaning of point (8) of Article 226, in respect of the single service provided by the travel agent shall be the travel agent's margin, that is to say, the difference between the total amount, exclusive of VAT, to be paid by the traveler and the actual cost to the travel agent of supplies of goods or services provided by other taxable persons, where those transactions are for the direct benefit of the traveler.

Article 309

If transactions entrusted by the travel agent to other taxable persons are performed by such persons outside the Community, the supply of services carried out by the travel agent shall be treated as an intermediary activity exempted pursuant to Article 153.

If the transactions are performed both inside and outside the Community, only that part of the travel agent's service relating to transactions outside the Community may be exempted.

Article 310

VAT charged to the travel agent by other taxable persons in respect of transactions which are referred to in Article 307 and which are for the direct benefit of the traveler shall not be deductible or refundable in any Member State.

Chapter 4 Special Arrangements for Second-Hand Goods, Works of Art, Collectors' Items and Antiques

Section 1: Definitions

Article 311

1. For the purposes of this Chapter, and without prejudice to other Community provisions, the following definitions shall apply:

    (1) "second-hand goods" means movable tangible property that is suitable for further use as it is or after repair, other than works of art, collectors' items or antiques and other than precious metals or precious stones as defined by the Member States;

    (2) "works of art" means the objects listed in Annex IX, Part A;

    (3) "collectors' items" means the objects listed in Annex IX, Part B;

    (4) "antiques" means the objects listed in Annex IX, Part C;

    (5) "taxable dealer" means any taxable person who, in the course of his economic activity and with a view to resale, purchases, or applies for the purposes of his business, or imports, second-hand goods, works of art, collectors' items or antiques, whether that taxable person is acting for himself or on behalf of another person pursuant to a contract under which commission is payable on purchase or sale;

    (6) "organizer of a sale by public auction" means any taxable person who, in the course of his economic activity, offers goods for sale by public auction with a view to handing them over to the highest bidder;

    (7) "principal of an organizer of a sale by public auction" means any person who transmits goods to an organizer of a sale by public auction pursuant to a contract under which commission is payable on a sale.

2. Member States need not regard as works of art the objects listed in points (5), (6) or (7) of Annex IX, Part A.

3. The contract under which commission is payable on a sale, referred to in point (7) of paragraph 1, must provide that the organizer of the sale is to put up the goods for public auction in his own name but on behalf of his principal and that he is to hand over the goods, in his own name but on behalf of his principal, to the highest bidder at the public auction.

Section 2: Special arrangements for taxable dealers

Subsection 1: Margin scheme

Article 312

For the purposes of this Subsection, the following definitions shall apply:

(1) "selling price" means everything which constitutes the consideration obtained or to be obtained by the taxable dealer from the customer or from a third party, including subsidies directly linked to the transaction, taxes, duties, levies and charges and incidental expenses such as commission, packaging, transport and insurance costs charged by the taxable dealer to the customer, but excluding the amounts referred to in Article 79;

(2) "purchase price" means everything which constitutes the consideration, for the purposes of point (1), obtained or to be obtained from the taxable dealer by his supplier.

Article 313

1. In respect of the supply of second-hand goods, works of art, collectors' items or antiques carried out by taxable dealers, Member States shall apply a special scheme for taxing the profit margin made by the taxable dealer, in accordance with the provisions of this Subsection.

2. Pending introduction of the definitive arrangements referred to in Article 402, the scheme referred to in paragraph 1 of this Article shall not apply to the supply of new means of transport, carried out in accordance with the conditions specified in Article 138(1) and (2)(a).

Article 314

The margin scheme shall apply to the supply by a taxable dealer of second-hand goods, works of art, collectors' items or antiques where those goods have been supplied to him within the Community by one of the following persons:

(a) a non-taxable person;

(b) another taxable person, in so far as the supply of goods by that other taxable person is exempt pursuant to Article 136;

(c) another taxable person, in so far as the supply of goods by that other taxable person is covered by the exemption for small enterprises provided for in Articles 282 to 292 and involves capital goods;

(d) another taxable dealer, in so far as VAT has been applied to the supply of goods by that other taxable dealer in accordance with this margin scheme.

Article 315

The taxable amount in respect of the supply of goods as referred to in Article 314 shall be the profit margin made by the taxable dealer, less the amount of VAT relating to the profit margin.

The profit margin of the taxable dealer shall be equal to the difference between the selling price charged by the taxable dealer for the goods and the purchase price.

Article 316

1. Member States shall grant taxable dealers the right to opt for application of the margin scheme to the following transactions:

    (a) the supply of works of art, collectors' items or antiques, which the taxable dealer has imported himself;

    (b) the supply of works of art supplied to the taxable dealer by their creators or their successors in title;

    (c) the supply of works of art supplied to the taxable dealer by a taxable person other than a taxable dealer where the reduced rate has been applied to that supply pursuant to Article 103.

2. Member States shall lay down the detailed rules for exercise of the option provided for in paragraph 1, which shall in any event cover a period of at least two calendar years.

Article 317

If a taxable dealer exercises the option under Article 316, the taxable amount shall be determined in accordance with Article 315.

In respect of the supply of works of art, collectors' items or antiques which the taxable dealer has imported himself, the purchase price to be taken into account in calculating the profit margin shall be equal to the taxable amount on importation, determined in accordance with Articles 85 to 89, plus the VAT due or paid on importation.

Article 318

1. In order to simplify the procedure for collecting the tax and after consulting the VAT Committee, Member States may provide that, for certain transactions or for certain categories of taxable dealers, the taxable amount in respect of supplies of goods subject to the margin scheme is to be determined for each tax period during which the taxable dealer must submit the VAT return referred to in Article 250.

In the event that such provision is made in accordance with the first subparagraph, the taxable amount in respect of supplies of goods to which the same rate of VAT is applied shall be the total profit margin made by the taxable dealer less the amount of VAT relating to that margin.

2. The total profit margin shall be equal to the difference between the following two amounts:

   (a) the total value of supplies of goods subject to the margin scheme and carried out by the taxable dealer during the tax period covered by the return, that is to say, the total of the selling prices;

   (b) the total value of purchases of goods, as referred to in Article 314, effected by the taxable dealer during the tax period covered by the return, that is to say, the total of the purchase prices.

3. Member States shall take the measures necessary to ensure that the taxable dealers referred to in paragraph 1 do not enjoy unjustified advantage or sustain unjustified harm.

Article 319

The taxable dealer may apply the normal VAT arrangements to any supply covered by the margin scheme.

Article 320

1. Where the taxable dealer applies the normal VAT arrangements to the supply of a work of art, a collectors' item or an antique which he has imported himself, he shall be entitled to deduct from the VAT for which he is liable the VAT due or paid on the import.

Where the taxable dealer applies the normal VAT arrangements to the supply of a work of art supplied to him by its creator, or the creator's successors in title, or by a taxable person other than a taxable dealer, he shall be entitled to deduct from the VAT for which he is liable the VAT due or paid in respect of the work of art supplied to him.

2. A right of deduction shall arise at the time when the VAT due on the supply in respect of which the taxable dealer opts for application of the normal VAT arrangements becomes chargeable.

Article 321

If carried out in accordance with the conditions specified in Articles 146, 147, 148 or 151, the supply of second-hand goods, works of art, collectors' items or antiques subject to the margin scheme shall be exempt.

Article 322

In so far as goods are used for the purpose of supplies carried out by him and subject to the margin scheme, the taxable dealer may not deduct the following from the VAT for which he is liable:

   (a) the VAT due or paid in respect of works of art, collectors' items or antiques which he has imported himself;

(b) the VAT due or paid in respect of works of art which have been, or are to be, supplied to him by their creator or by the creator's successors in title;

(c) the VAT due or paid in respect of works of art which have been, or are to be, supplied to him by a taxable person other than a taxable dealer.

Article 323

Taxable persons may not deduct from the VAT for which they are liable the VAT due or paid in respect of goods which have been, or are to be, supplied to them by a taxable dealer, in so far as the supply of those goods by the taxable dealer is subject to the margin scheme.

Article 324

Where the taxable dealer applies both the normal VAT arrangements and the margin scheme, he must show separately in his accounts the transactions falling under each of those arrangements, in accordance with the rules laid down by the Member States.

Article 325

The taxable dealer may not enter separately on the invoices which he issues the VAT relating to supplies of goods to which he applies the margin scheme.

Subsection 2: Transitional arrangements for second-hand means of transport

Article 326

Member States which, at 31 December 1992, were applying special tax arrangements other than the margin scheme to the supply by taxable dealers of second-hand means of transport may, pending introduction of the definitive arrangements referred to in Article 402, continue to apply those arrangements in so far as they comply with, or are adjusted to comply with, the conditions laid down in this Subsection.

Denmark is authorized to introduce tax arrangements as referred to in the first paragraph.

Article 327

1. These transitional arrangements shall apply to supplies of second-hand means of transport carried out by taxable dealers, and subject to the margin scheme.

2. These transitional arrangements shall not apply to the supply of new means of transport carried out in accordance with the conditions specified in Article 138(1) and (2)(a).

3. For the purposes of paragraph 1, the land vehicles, vessels and aircraft referred to in point (a) of Article 2(2) shall be regarded as "second-hand means of transport" where

they are second-hand goods which do not meet the conditions necessary to be regarded as new means of transport.

Article 328

The VAT due in respect of each supply referred to in Article 327 shall be equal to the amount of VAT that would have been due if that supply had been subject to the normal VAT arrangements, less the amount of VAT regarded as being incorporated by the taxable dealer in the purchase price of the means of transport.

Article 329

The VAT regarded as being incorporated by the taxable dealer in the purchase price of the means of transport shall be calculated in accordance with the following method:

(a) the purchase price to be taken into account shall be the purchase price within the meaning of point (2) of Article 312;

(b) that purchase price paid by the taxable dealer shall be deemed to include the VAT that would have been due if the taxable dealer's supplier had applied the normal VAT arrangements to the supply;

(c) the rate to be taken into account shall be the rate applicable, pursuant to Article 93, in the Member State in the territory of which the place of the supply to the taxable dealer, as determined in accordance with Articles 31 and 32, is deemed to be situated.

Article 330

The VAT due in respect of each supply of means of transport as referred to in Article 327(1), determined in accordance with Article 328, may not be less than the amount of VAT that would be due if that supply were subject to the margin scheme.

Member States may provide that, if the supply is subject to the margin scheme, the margin may not be less than 10 % of the selling price within the meaning of point (1) of Article 312.

Article 331

Taxable persons may not deduct from the VAT for which they are liable the VAT due or paid in respect of second-hand means of transport supplied to them by a taxable dealer, in so far as the supply of those goods by the taxable dealer is subject to VAT in accordance with these transitional arrangements.

Article 332

The taxable dealer may not enter separately on the invoices he issues the VAT relating to supplies to which he applies these transitional arrangements.

Section 3: Special arrangements for sales by public auction

Article 333

1. Member States may, in accordance with the provisions of this Section, apply special arrangements for taxation of the profit margin made by an organizer of a sale by public auction in respect of the supply of second-hand goods, works of art, collectors' items or antiques by that organizer, acting in his own name and on behalf of the persons referred to in Article 334, pursuant to a contract under which commission is payable on the sale of those goods by public auction.

2. The arrangements referred to in paragraph 1 shall not apply to the supply of new means of transport, carried out in accordance with the conditions specified in Article 138(1) and (2)(a).

Article 334

These special arrangements shall apply to supplies carried out by an organizer of a sale by public auction, acting in his own name, on behalf of one of the following persons:

(a) a non-taxable person;

(b) another taxable person, in so far as the supply of goods, carried out by that taxable person in accordance with a contract under which commission is payable on a sale, is exempt pursuant to Article 136;

(c) another taxable person, in so far as the supply of goods, carried out by that taxable person in accordance with a contract under which commission is payable on a sale, is covered by the exemption for small enterprises provided for in Articles 282 to 292 and involves capital goods;

(d) a taxable dealer, in so far as the supply of goods, carried out by that taxable dealer in accordance with a contract under which commission is payable on a sale, is subject to VAT in accordance with the margin scheme.

Article 335

The supply of goods to a taxable person who is an organizer of sales by public auction shall be regarded as taking place when the sale of those goods by public auction takes place.

Article 336

The taxable amount in respect of each supply of goods referred to in this Section shall be the total amount invoiced in accordance with Article 339 to the purchaser by the organizer of the sale by public auction, less the following:

(a) the net amount paid or to be paid by the organizer of the sale by public auction to his principal, as determined in accordance with Article 337;

(b) the amount of the VAT payable by the organizer of the sale by public auction in respect of his supply.

Article 337

The net amount paid or to be paid by the organizer of the sale by public auction to his principal shall be equal to the difference between the auction price of the goods and the amount of the commission obtained or to be obtained by the organizer of the sale by public auction from his principal pursuant to the contract under which commission is payable on the sale.

Article 338

Organizers of sales by public auction who supply goods in accordance with the conditions laid down in Articles 333 and 334 must indicate the following in their accounts, in suspense accounts:

(a) the amounts obtained or to be obtained from the purchaser of the goods;

(b) the amounts reimbursed or to be reimbursed to the vendor of the goods.

The amounts referred to in the first paragraph must be duly substantiated.

Article 339

The organizer of the sale by public auction must issue to the purchaser an invoice itemizing the following:

(a) the auction price of the goods;

(b) taxes, duties, levies and charges;

(c) incidental expenses, such as commission, packing, transport and insurance costs, charged by the organizer to the purchaser of the goods.

The invoice issued by the organizer of the sale by public auction must not indicate any VAT separately.

Article 340

1. The organizer of the sale by public auction to whom the goods have been transmitted pursuant to a contract under which commission is payable on a public auction sale must issue a statement to his principal.

The statement issued by the organizer of the sale by public auction must specify separately the amount of the transaction, that is to say, the auction price of the goods less the amount of the commission obtained or to be obtained from the principal.

2. The statement drawn up in accordance with paragraph 1 shall serve as the invoice which the principal, where he is a taxable person, must issue to the organizer of the sale by public auction in accordance with Article 220.

Article 341

Member States which apply the arrangements provided for in this Section shall also apply these arrangements to supplies of second-hand means of transport, as defined in Article 327(3), carried out by an organizer of sales by public auction, acting in his own name, pursuant to a contract under which commission is payable on the sale of those goods by public auction, on behalf of a taxable dealer, in so far as those supplies by that taxable dealer would be subject to VAT in accordance with the transitional arrangements for second-hand means of transport.

Section 4: Measures to prevent distortion of competition and tax evasion

Article 342

Member States may take measures concerning the right of deduction in order to ensure that the taxable dealers covered by special arrangements as provided for in Section 2 do not enjoy unjustified advantage or sustain unjustified harm.

Article 343

Acting unanimously on a proposal from the Commission, the Council may authorize any Member State to introduce special measures to combat tax evasion, pursuant to which the VAT due under the margin scheme may not be less than the amount of VAT which would be due if the profit margin were equal to a certain percentage of the selling price.

The percentage of the selling price shall be fixed in the light of the normal profit margins made by economic operators in the sector concerned.

Chapter 5 Special Scheme for Investment Gold

Section 1: General provisions

Article 344

1. For the purposes of this Directive, and without prejudice to other Community provisions, "investment gold" shall mean:

    (1) gold, in the form of a bar or a wafer of weights accepted by the bullion markets, of a purity equal to or greater than 995 thousandths, whether or not represented by securities;

    (2) gold coins of a purity equal to or greater than 900 thousandths and minted after 1800, which are or have been legal tender in the country of origin, and are normally sold at a price which does not exceed the open market value of the gold contained in the coins by more than 80 %.

2. Member States may exclude from this special scheme small bars or wafers of a weight of 1 g or less.

3. For the purposes of this Directive, the coins referred to in point (2) of paragraph 1 shall not be regarded as sold for numismatic interest.

Article 345

Starting in 1999, each Member State shall inform the Commission by 1 July each year of the coins meeting the criteria laid down in point (2) of Article 344(1) which are traded in that Member State. The Commission shall, before 1 December each year, publish a comprehensive list of those coins in the "C" series of the Official Journal of the European Union. Coins included in the published list shall be deemed to fulfill those criteria throughout the year for which the list is published.

Section 2: Exemption from VAT

Article 346

Member States shall exempt from VAT the supply, the intra-Community acquisition and the importation of investment gold, including investment gold represented by certificates for allocated or unallocated gold or traded on gold accounts and including, in particular, gold loans and swaps, involving a right of ownership or claim in respect of investment gold, as well as transactions concerning investment gold involving futures and forward contracts leading to a transfer of right of ownership or claim in respect of investment gold.

Article 347

Member States shall exempt the services of agents who act in the name and on behalf of another person, when they take part in the supply of investment gold for their principal.

Section 3: Taxation option

Article 348

Member States shall allow taxable persons who produce investment gold or transform gold into investment gold the right to opt for the taxation of supplies of investment gold to another taxable person which would otherwise be exempt pursuant to Article 346.

Article 349

1. Member States may allow taxable persons who, in the course of their economic activity, normally supply gold for industrial purposes, the right to opt for the taxation of supplies of gold bars or wafers, as referred to in point (1) of Article 344(1), to another taxable person, which would otherwise be exempt pursuant to Article 346.

2. Member States may restrict the scope of the option provided for in paragraph 1.

Article 350

Where the supplier has exercised the right under Articles 348 and 349 to opt for taxation, Member States shall allow the agent to opt for taxation of the services referred to in Article 347.

Article 351

Member States shall lay down detailed rules for the exercise of the options provided for in this Section, and shall inform the Commission accordingly.

Section 4: Transactions on a regulated gold bullion market

Article 352

Each Member State may, after consulting the VAT Committee, apply VAT to specific transactions relating to investment gold which take place in that Member State between taxable persons who are members of a gold bullion market regulated by the Member State concerned or between such a taxable person and another taxable person who is not a member of that market. However, the Member State may not apply VAT to supplies carried out in accordance with the conditions specified in Article 138 or to exports of investment gold.

Article 353

Member States which, pursuant to Article 352, tax transactions between taxable persons who are members of a regulated gold bullion market shall, for the purposes of simplification, authorize suspension of the tax to be collected and relieve taxable persons of the accounting requirements in respect of VAT.

Section 5: Special rights and obligations for traders in investment gold

Article 354

Where his subsequent supply of investment gold is exempt pursuant to this Chapter, the taxable person shall be entitled to deduct the following:

- (a) the VAT due or paid in respect of investment gold supplied to him by a person who has exercised the right of option under Articles 348 and 349 or supplied to him in accordance with Section 4;
- (b) the VAT due or paid in respect of a supply to him, or in respect of an intra-Community acquisition or importation carried out by him, of gold other than investment gold which is subsequently transformed by him or on his behalf into investment gold;
- (c) the VAT due or paid in respect of services supplied to him consisting in a change of form, weight or purity of gold including investment gold.

Article 355

Taxable persons who produce investment gold or transform gold into investment gold shall be entitled to deduct the VAT due or paid by them in respect of the supply, intra-Community acquisition or importation of goods or services linked to the production or transformation of that gold, as if the subsequent supply of the gold exempted pursuant to Article 346 were taxed.

Article 356

1. Member States shall ensure that traders in investment gold keep, as a minimum, accounts of all substantial transactions in investment gold and keep the documents which enable the customers in such transactions to be identified.

Traders shall keep the information referred to in the first subparagraph for a period of at least five years.

2. Member States may accept equivalent obligations under measures adopted pursuant to other Community legislation, such as Directive 2005/60/EC of the European Parliament and of the Council of 26 October 2005 on the prevention of the use of the financial system for the purpose of money laundering and terrorist financing, to comply with the requirements under paragraph 1.

3. Member States may lay down obligations which are more stringent, in particular as regards the keeping of special records or special accounting requirements.

Chapter 6 Special Scheme for Non-Established Taxable Persons supplying Electronic Services to Non-Taxable Persons

Section 1: General provisions

Article 357

This Chapter shall apply until 31 December 2014.

Article 358

For the purposes of this Chapter, and without prejudice to other provisions, the following definitions shall apply:

(1) "non-established taxable person" means a taxable person who has not established his business in the territory of the Community and who has no fixed establishment there and who is not otherwise required to be identified pursuant to Article 214;

(2) "electronic services" and "electronically supplied services" mean the services referred to in point (k) of the first paragraph of Article 59;

(3) "Member State of identification" means the Member State which the non-established taxable person chooses to contact to state when his activity as a taxable person within the territory of the Community commences in accordance with the provisions of this Chapter;

(4) Member State of consumption" means the Member State in which, pursuant to Article 58, the supply of the electronic services is deemed to take place;

(5) "VAT return" means the statement containing the information necessary to establish the amount of VAT due in each Member State.

Section 2: Special scheme for electronically supplied services

Article 359

Member States shall permit any non-established taxable person supplying electronic services to a non-taxable person who is established in a Member State or who has his permanent address or usually resides in a Member State, to use this special scheme. This scheme applies to all electronic services supplied in the Community.

Article 360

The non-established taxable person shall state to the Member State of identification when he commences or ceases his activity as a taxable person, or changes that activity in such a way that he no longer meets the conditions necessary for use of this special scheme. He shall communicate that information electronically.

Article 361

1. The information which the non-established taxable person must provide to the Member State of identification when he commences a taxable activity shall contain the following details:

    (a) name;

    (b) postal address;

    (c) electronic addresses, including websites;

    (d) national tax number, if any;

    (e) a statement that the person is not identified for VAT purposes within the Community.

2. The non-established taxable person shall notify the Member State of identification of any changes in the information provided.

Article 362

The Member State of identification shall allocate to the non-established taxable person an individual VAT identification number and shall notify him of that number by electronic means. On the basis of the information used for that identification, Member States of consumption may have recourse to their own identification systems.

Article 363

The Member State of identification shall strike the non-established taxable person from the identification register in the following cases:

   (a) if he notifies that Member State that he no longer supplies electronic services;

   (b) if it may otherwise be assumed that his taxable activities have ceased;

   (c) if he no longer meets the conditions necessary for use of this special scheme;

   (d) if he persistently fails to comply with the rules relating to this special scheme.

Article 364

The non-established taxable person shall submit by electronic means to the Member State of identification a VAT return for each calendar quarter, whether or not electronic services have been supplied. The VAT return shall be submitted within 20 days following the end of the tax period covered by the return.

Article 365

The VAT return shall show the identification number and, for each Member State of consumption in which VAT is due, the total value, exclusive of VAT, of supplies of electronic services carried out during the tax period and the total amount of the corresponding VAT. The applicable rates of VAT and the total VAT due must also be indicated on the return.

Article 366

1. The VAT return shall be made out in euro.

Member States which have not adopted the euro may require the VAT return to be made out in their national currency. If the supplies have been made in other currencies, the non-established taxable person shall, for the purposes of completing the VAT return, use the exchange rate applying on the last day of the tax period.

2. The conversion shall be made by applying the exchange rates published by the European Central Bank for that day, or, if there is no publication on that day, on the next day of publication.

Article 367

The non-established taxable person shall pay the VAT when submitting the VAT return.

Payment shall be made to a bank account denominated in euro, designated by the Member State of identification. Member States which have not adopted the euro may require payment to be made to a bank account denominated in their own currency.

Article 368

The non-established taxable person making use of this special scheme may not deduct VAT pursuant to Article 168 of this Directive. Notwithstanding Article 1(1) of Directive 86/560/EEC, the taxable person in question shall be refunded in accordance with the said Directive. Articles 2(2) and (3) and Article 4(2) of Directive 86/560/EEC shall not apply to refunds relating to electronic services covered by this special scheme.

Article 369

1. The non-established taxable person shall keep records of the transactions covered by this special scheme. Those records must be sufficiently detailed to enable the tax authorities of the Member State of consumption to verify that the VAT return is correct.

2. The records referred to in paragraph 1 must be made available electronically on request to the Member State of identification and to the Member State of consumption.

Those records must be kept for a period of ten years from the end of the year during which the transaction was carried out.

Title XIII Derogations

Chapter 1 Derogations Applying Until the Adoption of Definitive Arrangements

Section 1: Derogations for States which were members of the Community on 1 January 1978

Article 370

Member States which, at 1 January 1978, taxed the transactions listed in Annex X, Part A, may continue to tax those transactions.

Article 371

Member States which, at 1 January 1978, exempted the transactions listed in Annex X, Part B, may continue to exempt those transactions, in accordance with the conditions applying in the Member State concerned on that date.

Article 372

Member States which, at 1 January 1978, applied provisions derogating from the principle of immediate deduction laid down in the first paragraph of Article 179 may continue to apply those provisions.

Article 373

Member States which, at 1 January 1978, applied provisions derogating from Article 28 or from point (c) of the first paragraph of Article 79 may continue to apply those provisions.

Article 374

By way of derogation from Articles 169 and 309, Member States which, at 1 January 1978, exempted, without deductibility of the VAT paid at the preceding stage, the services of travel agents, as referred to in Article 309, may continue to exempt those services. That derogation shall apply also in respect of travel agents acting in the name and on behalf of the traveler.

Section 2: Derogations for States which acceded to the Community after 1 January 1978

Article 375

Greece may continue to exempt the transactions listed in points (2), (8), (9), (11) and (12) of Annex X, Part B, in accordance with the conditions applying in that Member State on 1 January 1987.

Article 376

Spain may continue to exempt the supply of services performed by authors, listed in point (2) of Annex X, Part B, and the transactions listed in points (11) and (12) of Annex X, Part B, in accordance with the conditions applying in that Member State on 1 January 1993.

Article 377

Portugal may continue to exempt the transactions listed in points (2), (4), (7), (9), (10) and (13) of Annex X, Part B, in accordance with the conditions applying in that Member State on 1 January 1989.

Article 378

1. Austria may continue to tax the transactions listed in point (2) of Annex X, Part A.

2. For as long as the same exemptions are applied in any of the Member States which were members of the Community on 31 December 1994, Austria may, in accordance with the conditions applying in that Member State on the date of its accession, continue to exempt the following transactions:

    (a) the transactions listed in points (5) and (9) of Annex X, Part B;

    (b) with deductibility of the VAT paid at the preceding stage, all parts of international passenger transport operations, carried out by air, sea or inland waterway, other than passenger transport operations on Lake Constance.

Article 379

1. Finland may continue to tax the transactions listed in point (2) of Annex X, Part A, for as long as the same transactions are taxed in any of the Member States which were members of the Community on 31 December 1994.

2. Finland may, in accordance with the conditions applying in that Member State on the date of its accession, continue to exempt the supply of services by authors, artists and performers, listed in point (2) of Annex X, Part B, and the transactions listed in points (5), (9) and (10) of Annex X, Part B, for as long as the same exemptions are applied in any of the Member States which were members of the Community on 31 December 1994.

Article 380

Sweden may, in accordance with the conditions applying in that Member State on the date of its accession, continue to exempt the supply of services by authors, artists and performers, listed in point (2) of Annex X, Part B, and the transactions listed in points (1), (9) and (10) of Annex X, Part B, for as long as the same exemptions are applied in any of the Member States which were members of the Community on 31 December 1994.

Article 381

The Czech Republic may, in accordance with the conditions applying in that Member State on the date of its accession, continue to exempt the international transport of passengers, as referred to in point (10) of Annex X, Part B, for as long as the same exemption is applied in any of the Member States which were members of the Community on 30 April 2004.

Article 382

Estonia may, in accordance with the conditions applying in that Member State on the date of its accession, continue to exempt the international transport of passengers, as referred to in point (10) of Annex X, Part B, for as long as the same exemption is applied in any of the Member States which were members of the Community on 30 April 2004.

Article 383

Cyprus may, in accordance with the conditions applying in that Member State on the date of its accession, continue to exempt the following transactions:

(a) the supply of building land referred to in point (9) of Annex X, Part B, until 31 December 2007;

(b) the international transport of passengers, as referred to in point (10) of Annex X, Part B, for as long as the same exemption is applied in any of the Member States which were members of the Community on 30 April 2004.

Article 384

For as long as the same exemptions are applied in any of the Member States which were members of the Community on 30 April 2004, Latvia may, in accordance with the conditions applying in that Member State on the date of its accession, continue to exempt the following transactions:

(a) the supply of services by authors, artists and performers, as referred to in point (2) of Annex X, Part B;

(b) the international transport of passengers, as referred to in point (10) of Annex X, Part B.

Article 385

Lithuania may, in accordance with the conditions applying in that Member State on the date of its accession, continue to exempt the international transport of passengers, as referred to in point (10) of Annex X, Part B, for as long as the same exemption is applied in any of the Member States which were members of the Community on 30 April 2004.

Article 386

Hungary may, in accordance with the conditions applying in that Member State on the date of its accession, continue to exempt the international transport of passengers, as referred to in point (10) of Annex X, Part B, for as long as the same exemption is applied in any of the Member States which were members of the Community on 30 April 2004.

Article 387

For as long as the same exemptions are applied in any of the Member States which were members of the Community on 30 April 2004, Malta may, in accordance with the conditions applying in that Member State on the date of its accession, continue to exempt the following transactions:

- (a) without deductibility of the VAT paid at the preceding stage, the supply of water by a body governed by public law, as referred to in point (8) of Annex X, Part B;
- (b) without deductibility of the VAT paid at the preceding stage, the supply of buildings and building land, as referred to in point (9) of Annex X, Part B;
- (c) with deductibility of the VAT paid at the preceding stage, inland passenger transport, international passenger transport and domestic inter-island sea passenger transport, as referred to in point (10) of Annex X, Part B.

Article 388

Poland may, in accordance with the conditions applying in that Member State on the date of its accession, continue to exempt the international transport of passengers, as referred to in point (10) of Annex X, Part B, for as long as the same exemption is applied in any of the Member States which were members of the Community on 30 April 2004.

Article 389

Slovenia may, in accordance with the conditions applying in that Member State on the date of its accession, continue to exempt the international transport of passengers, as referred to in point (10) of Annex X, Part B, for as long as the same exemption is applied in any of the Member States which were members of the Community on 30 April 2004.

Article 390

Slovakia may, in accordance with the conditions applying in that Member State on the date of its accession, continue to exempt the international transport of passengers, as referred to in point (10) of Annex X, Part B, for as long as the same exemption is applied in any of the Member States which were members of the Community on 30 April 2004.

Article 390a

Bulgaria may, in accordance with the conditions applying in that Member State on the date of its accession, continue to exempt the international transport of passengers as referred to in point 10 of Annex X, Part B, for as long as the same exemption is applied in any of the Member States which were members of the Community on 31 December 2006.

Article 390b

Romania may, in accordance with the conditions applying in that Member State on the date of its accession, continue to exempt the international transport of passengers, as referred to in point 10 of Annex X, Part B, for as long as the same exemption is applied in any of the Member States which were members of the Community on 31 December 2006.

Article 390c

Croatia may, in accordance with the conditions applying in that Member State on the date of its accession, continue to exempt the following transactions:

(a) the supply of building land, with or without buildings built on it, as referred to in point (j) of Article 135(1) and in point (9) of Annex X, Part B, non-renewable, until 31 December 2014;

(b) the international transport of passengers, as referred to in point (10) of Annex X, Part B, for as long as the same exemption is applied in any of the Member States which were members of the Union before the accession of Croatia.

Section 3: Provisions common to Sections 1 and 2

Article 391

Member States which exempt the transactions referred to in Articles 371, 375, 376 or 377, Article 378(2), Article 379(2) or Articles 380 to 390c may grant taxable persons the right to opt for taxation of those transactions.

Article 392

Member States may provide that, in respect of the supply of buildings and building land purchased for the purpose of resale by a taxable person for whom the VAT on the purchase was not deductible, the taxable amount shall be the difference between the selling price and the purchase price.

Article 393

1. With a view to facilitating the transition to the definitive arrangements referred to in Article 402, the Council shall, on the basis of a report from the Commission, review the situation with regard to the derogations provided for in Sections 1 and 2 and shall, acting in accordance with Article 93 of the Treaty decide whether any or all of those derogations is to be abolished.

2. By way of definitive arrangements, passenger transport shall be taxed in the Member State of departure for that part of the journey taking place within the Community, in accordance with the detailed rules to be laid down by the Council, acting in accordance with Article 93 of the Treaty.

Chapter 2 Derogations Subject to Authorization

Section 1: Simplification measures and measures to prevent tax evasion or avoidance

Article 394

Member States which, at 1 January 1977, applied special measures to simplify the procedure for collecting VAT or to prevent certain forms of tax evasion or avoidance may retain them provided that they have notified the Commission accordingly before 1 January 1978 and that such simplification measures comply with the criterion laid down in the second subparagraph of Article 395(1).

Article 395

1. The Council, acting unanimously on a proposal from the Commission, may authorize any Member State to introduce special measures for derogation from the provisions of this Directive, in order to simplify the procedure for collecting VAT or to prevent certain forms of tax evasion or avoidance.

Measures intended to simplify the procedure for collecting VAT may not, except to a negligible extent, affect the overall amount of the tax revenue of the Member State collected at the stage of final consumption.

2. A Member State wishing to introduce the measure referred to in paragraph 1 shall send an application to the Commission and provide it with all the necessary information. If the Commission considers that it does not have all the necessary information, it shall contact the Member State concerned within two months of receipt of the application and specify what additional information is required.

Once the Commission has all the information it considers necessary for appraisal of the request it shall within one month notify the requesting Member State accordingly and it shall transmit the request, in its original language, to the other Member States.

3. Within three months of giving the notification referred to in the second subparagraph of paragraph 2, the Commission shall present to the Council either an appropriate proposal or, should it object to the derogation requested, a communication setting out its objections.

4. The procedure laid down in paragraphs 2 and 3 shall, in any event, be completed within eight months of receipt of the application by the Commission.

5. In cases of imperative urgency as set out in Article 199b(1), the procedure laid down in paragraphs 2 and 3 shall be completed within six months of receipt of the application by the Commission.

Section 2: International Agreements

Article 396

1. The Council, acting unanimously on a proposal from the Commission, may authorize any Member State to conclude with a third country or an international body an agreement which may contain derogations from this Directive.

2. A Member State wishing to conclude an agreement as referred to in paragraph 1 shall send an application to the Commission and provide it with all the necessary information. If the Commission considers that it does not have all the necessary information, it shall contact the Member State concerned within two months of receipt of the application and specify what additional information is required.

Once the Commission has all the information it considers necessary for appraisal of the request it shall within one month notify the requesting Member State accordingly and it shall transmit the request, in its original language, to the other Member States.

3. Within three months of giving the notification referred to in the second subparagraph of paragraph 2, the Commission shall present to the Council either an appropriate proposal or, should it object to the derogation requested, a communication setting out its objections.

3. The procedure laid down in paragraphs 2 and 3 shall, in any event, be completed within eight months of receipt of the application by the Commission.

Title XIV - Miscellaneous

Chapter 1 Implementing Measures

Article 397

The Council, acting unanimously on a proposal from the Commission, shall adopt the measures necessary to implement this Directive.

Chapter 2 VAT Committee

Article 398

1. An advisory committee on value added tax, called "the VAT Committee", is set up.

2. The VAT Committee shall consist of representatives of the Member States and of the Commission.

The chairman of the Committee shall be a representative of the Commission.

Secretarial services for the Committee shall be provided by the Commission.

3. The VAT Committee shall adopt its own rules of procedure.

4. In addition to the points forming the subject of consultation pursuant to this Directive, the VAT Committee shall examine questions raised by its chairman, on his own initiative or at the request of the representative of a Member State, which concern the application of Community provisions on VAT.

Chapter 3 Conversion Rates

Article 399

Without prejudice to any other particular provisions, the equivalents in national currency of the amounts in euro specified in this Directive shall be determined on the basis of the euro conversion rate applicable on 1 January 1999. Member States having acceded to the European Union after that date, which have not adopted the euro as single currency, shall use the euro conversion rate applicable on the date of their accession.

Article 400

When converting the amounts referred to in Article 399 into national currencies, Member States may adjust the amounts resulting from that conversion either upwards or downwards by up to 10 %.

Chapter 4 Other Taxes, Duties and Charges

Article 401

Without prejudice to other provisions of Community law, this Directive shall not prevent a Member State from maintaining or introducing taxes on insurance contracts, taxes on betting and gambling, excise duties, stamp duties or, more generally, any taxes, duties or charges which cannot be characterized as turnover taxes, provided that the collecting of those taxes, duties or charges does not give rise, in trade between Member States, to formalities connected with the crossing of frontiers.

Title XV - Final Provisions

Chapter 1 Transitional Arrangements for the Taxation of Trade between Member States

Article 402

1. The arrangements provided for in this Directive for the taxation of trade between Member States are transitional and shall be replaced by definitive arrangements based in principle on the taxation in the Member State of origin of the supply of goods or services.

2. Having concluded, upon examination of the report referred to in Article 404, that the conditions for transition to the definitive arrangements are met, the Council shall, acting in accordance with Article 93 of the Treaty, adopt the provisions necessary for the entry into force and for the operation of the definitive arrangements.

Article 403

The Council shall, acting in accordance with Article 93 of the Treaty, adopt Directives appropriate for the purpose of supplementing the common system of VAT and, in particular, for the progressive restriction or the abolition of derogations from that system.

Article 404

Every four years starting from the adoption of this Directive, the Commission shall, on the basis of information obtained from the Member States, present a report to the European Parliament and to the Council on the operation of the common system of VAT in the Member States and, in particular, on the operation of the transitional arrangements for taxing trade between Member States. That report shall be accompanied, where appropriate, by proposals concerning the definitive arrangements.

Chapter 2 Transitional Measures applicable in the Context of Accession to the European Union

Article 405

For the purposes of this Chapter, the following definitions shall apply:

1. "Community" means the territory of the Community as defined in point (1) of Article 5 before the accession of new Member States;

2. "new Member States" means the territory of the Member States which acceded to the European Union after 1 January 1995, as defined for each of those Member States in point (2) of Article 5;

3. "enlarged Community" means the territory of the Community as defined in point (1) of Article 5 after the accession of new Member States.

Article 406

The provisions in force at the time the goods were placed under temporary importation arrangements with total exemption from import duty or under one of the arrangements or situations referred to in Article 156, or under similar arrangements or situations in one of the new Member States, shall continue to apply until the goods cease to be covered by these arrangements or situations after the date of accession, where the following conditions are met:

(a) the goods entered the Community or one of the new Member States before the date of accession;

(b) the goods were placed, on entry into the Community or one of the new Member States, under these arrangements or situations;

(c) the goods have not ceased to be covered by these arrangements or situations before the date of accession.

Article 407

The provisions in force at the time the goods were placed under customs transit arrangements shall continue to apply until the goods cease to be covered by these arrangements after the date of accession, where the following conditions are met:

(a) the goods were placed, before the date of accession, under customs transit arrangements;

(b) the goods have not ceased to be covered by these arrangements before the date of accession.

Article 408

1. The following shall be treated as an importation of goods where it is shown that the goods were in free circulation in one of the new Member States or in the Community:

    (a) the removal, including irregular removal, of goods from temporary importation arrangements under which they were placed before the date of accession under the conditions provided for in Article 406;

    (b) the removal, including irregular removal, of goods either from one of the arrangements or situations referred to in Article 156 or from similar arrangements or situations under which they were placed before the date of accession under the conditions provided for in Article 406;

    (c) the cessation of one of the arrangements referred to in Article 407, started before the date of accession in the territory of one of the new Member States, for the purposes of a supply of goods for consideration effected before that date in the territory of that Member State by a taxable person acting as such;

    (d) any irregularity or offence committed during customs transit arrangements started under the conditions referred to in point (c).

2. In addition to the case referred to in paragraph 1, the use after the date of accession within the territory of a Member State, by a taxable or non-taxable person, of goods supplied to him before the date of accession within the territory of the Community or one of the new Member States shall be treated as an importation of goods where the following conditions are met:

    (a) the supply of those goods has been exempted, or was likely to be exempted, either under points (a) and (b) of Article 146(1) or under a similar provision in the new Member States;

    (b) the goods were not imported into one of the new Member States or into the Community before the date of accession.

Article 409

In the cases referred to in Article 408(1), the place of import within the meaning of Article 61 shall be the Member State within whose territory the goods cease to be covered by the arrangements or situations under which they were placed before the date of accession.

Article 410

1. By way of derogation from Article 71, the importation of goods within the meaning of Article 408 shall terminate without the occurrence of a chargeable event if one of the following conditions is met:

    (a) the imported goods are dispatched or transported outside the enlarged Community;

    (b) the imported goods within the meaning of Article 408(1)(a) are other than means of transport and are redispatched or transported to the Member State from which they were exported and to the person who exported them;

    (c) the imported goods within the meaning of Article 408(1)(a) are means of transport which were acquired or imported before the date of accession in accordance with the general conditions of taxation in force on the domestic market of one of the new Member States or of one of the Member States of the Community or which have not been subject, by reason of their exportation, to any exemption from, or refund of, VAT.

2. The condition referred to in paragraph 1(c) shall be deemed to be fulfilled in the following cases:

    (a) when the date of first entry into service of the means of transport was more than eight years before the accession to the European Union.

    (b) when the amount of tax due by reason of the importation is insignificant.

Chapter 3 Transposition and Entry Into Force

Article 411

1. Directive 67/227/EEC and Directive 77/388/EEC are repealed, without prejudice to the obligations of the Member States concerning the time-limits, listed in Annex XI, Part B, for the transposition into national law and the implementation of those Directives.

2. References to the repealed Directives shall be construed as references to this Directive and shall be read in accordance with the correlation table in Annex XII.

Article 412

1. Member States shall bring into force the laws, regulations and administrative provisions necessary to comply with Article 2(3), Article 44, Article 59(1), Article 399 and Annex III, point (18) with effect from 1 January 2008. They shall forthwith communicate to the Commission the text of those provisions and a correlation table between those provisions and this Directive.

When Member States adopt those provisions, they shall contain a reference to this Directive or be accompanied by such a reference on the occasion of their official publication. Member States shall determine how such reference is to be made.

2. Member States shall communicate to the Commission the text of the main provisions of national law which they adopt in the field covered by this Directive.

Article 413

This Directive shall enter into force on 1 January 2007.

Article 414

This Directive is addressed to the Member States.

Annex I

List of the Activities referred to in the Third subparagraph of article 13(1)

(1) Telecommunications services;

(2) supply of water, gas, electricity and thermal energy;

(3) transport of goods;

(4) port and airport services;

(5) passenger transport;

(6) supply of new goods manufactured for sale;

(7) transactions in respect of agricultural products, carried out by agricultural intervention agencies pursuant to Regulations on the common organization of the market in those products;

(8) organization of trade fairs and exhibitions;

(9) warehousing;

(10) activities of commercial publicity bodies;

(11) activities of travel agents;

(12) running of staff shops, cooperatives and industrial canteens and similar institutions;

(13) activities carried out by radio and television bodies in so far as these are not exempt pursuant to Article 132(1)(q).

RECAST VAT DIRECTIVE

Annex II

Indicative List of the Electronically Supplied Services referred to in article 58 and point (k) of the first paragraph of article 59

(1) Website supply, web-hosting, distance maintenance of programs and equipment;

(2) supply of software and updating thereof;

(3) supply of images, text and information and making available of databases;

(4) supply of music, films and games, including games of chance and gambling games, and of political, cultural, artistic, sporting, scientific and entertainment broadcasts and events;

(5) supply of distance teaching.

Annex III

List of Supplies of Goods and Services to which the Reduced Rates referred to in article 98 may be applied

(1) Foodstuffs (including beverages but excluding alcoholic beverages) for human and animal consumption; live animals, seeds, plants and ingredients normally intended for use in the preparation of foodstuffs; products normally used to supplement foodstuffs or as a substitute for foodstuffs;

(2) supply of water;

(3) pharmaceutical products of a kind normally used for health care, prevention of illnesses and as treatment for medical and veterinary purposes, including products used for contraception and sanitary protection;

(4) medical equipment, aids and other appliances normally intended to alleviate or treat disability, for the exclusive personal use of the disabled, including the repair of such goods, and supply of children's car seats;

(5) transport of passengers and their accompanying luggage;

(6) supply, including on loan by libraries, of books on all physical means of support (including brochures, leaflets and similar printed matter, children's picture, drawing or coloring books, music printed or in manuscript form, maps and hydrographic or similar charts), newspapers and periodicals, other than material wholly or predominantly devoted to advertising;

(7) admission to shows, theatres, circuses, fairs, amusement parks, concerts, museums, zoos, cinemas, exhibitions and similar cultural events and facilities;

(8) reception of radio and television broadcasting services;

(9) supply of services by writers, composers and performing artists, or of the royalties due to them;

(10) provision, construction, renovation and alteration of housing, as part of a social policy;

(10a) renovation and repairing of private dwellings, excluding materials which account for a significant part of the value of the service supplied;

(10b) window-cleaning and cleaning in private households;

(11) supply of goods and services of a kind normally intended for use in agricultural production but excluding capital goods such as machinery or buildings;

(12) accommodation provided in hotels and similar establishments, including the provision of holiday accommodation and the letting of places on camping or caravan sites;

(12a) restaurant and catering services, it being possible to exclude the supply of (alcoholic and/or non-alcoholic) beverages;

(13) admission to sporting events;

(14) use of sporting facilities;

(15) supply of goods and services by organizations recognized as being devoted to social wellbeing by Member States and engaged in welfare or social security work, in so far as those transactions are not exempt pursuant to Articles 132, 135 and 136;

(16) supply of services by undertakers and cremation services, and the supply of goods related thereto;

(17) provision of medical and dental care and thermal treatment in so far as those services are not exempt pursuant to points (b) to (e) of Article 132(1);

(18) supply of services provided in connection with street cleaning, refuse collection and waste treatment, other than the supply of such services by bodies referred to in Article 13.

(19) minor repairing of bicycles, shoes and leather goods, clothing and household linen (including mending and alteration);

(20) domestic care services such as home help and care of young, elderly, sick or disabled;

(21) hairdressing.

Annex IV

[Deleted]

RECAST VAT DIRECTIVE

Annex V

Categories of Goods covered by Warehousing Arrangements other than Customs Warehousing as provided for under article 160(2)

	CN-code	Description of goods
(1)	0701	Potatoes
(2)	071120	Olives
(3)	0801	Coconuts, Brazil nuts and cashew nuts
(4)	0802	Other nuts
(5)	09011100 09011200	Coffee, not roasted
(6)	0902	Tea
(7)	1001 to 1005 1007 to 1008	Cereals
(9)	1006	Husked rice
(8)	1201 to 1207	Grains and oil seeds (including soya beans) and oleaginous fruits
(10)	1507 to 1515	Vegetable oils and fats and their fractions, whether or not refined, but not chemically modified
(11)	170111 170112	Raw sugar
(12)	1801	Cocoa beans, whole or broken, raw or roasted
(13)	2709 2710 271112 271113	Mineral oils (including propane and butane; also including crude petroleum oils)
(14)	Chapters 28 and 29	Chemicals in bulk
(15)	4001 4002	Rubber, in primary forms or in plates, sheets or strip
(16)	5101	Wool
(17)	7106	Silver
(18)	71101100 71102100 71103100	Platinum (palladium, rhodium)
(19)	7402 7403 7405 7408	Copper
(20)	7502	Nickel
(21)	7601	Aluminium
(22)	7801	Lead
(23)	7901	Zinc
(24)	8001	Tin
(25)	ex811292 ex811299	Indium

Annex VI

List of Supplies of Goods and Services as referred to in point (d) of article 199(1)

(1) Supply of ferrous and non ferrous waste, scrap, and used materials including that of semi-finished products resulting from the processing, manufacturing or melting down of ferrous and non-ferrous metals and their alloys;

(2) supply of ferrous and non-ferrous semi-processed products and certain associated processing services;

(3) supply of residues and other recyclable materials consisting of ferrous and non-ferrous metals, their alloys, slag, ash, scale and industrial residues containing metals or their alloys and supply of selection, cutting, fragmenting and pressing services of these products;

(4) supply of, and certain processing services relating to, ferrous and non-ferrous waste as well as parings, scrap, waste and used and recyclable material consisting of cullet, glass, paper, paperboard and board, rags, bone, leather, imitation leather, parchment, raw hides and skins, tendons and sinews, twine, cordage, rope, cables, rubber and plastic;

(5) supply of the materials referred to in this annex after processing in the form of cleaning, polishing, selection, cutting, fragmenting, pressing or casting into ingots;

(6) supply of scrap and waste from the working of base materials.

Annex VII

List of the Agricultural Production Activities referred to in point (4) of article 295(1)

(1) Crop production:

    (a) general agriculture, including viticulture;

    (b) growing of fruit (including olives) and of vegetables, flowers and ornamental plants, both in the open and under glass;

    (c) production of mushrooms, spices, seeds and propagating materials;

    (d) running of nurseries;

(2) stock farming together with cultivation:

    (a) general stock farming;

    (b) poultry farming;

    (c) rabbit farming;

    (d) beekeeping;

    (e) silkworm farming;

    (f) snail farming;

(3) forestry;

(4) fisheries:

    (a) freshwater fishing;

    (b) fish farming;

    (c) breeding of mussels, oysters and other mollusks and crustaceans;

    (d) frog farming.

Annex VIII

Indicative List of the Agricultural Services referred to in point (5) of article 295(1)

(1) Field work, reaping and mowing, threshing, baling, collecting, harvesting, sowing and planting;

(2) packing and preparation for market, such as drying, cleaning, grinding, disinfecting and ensilage of agricultural products;

(3) storage of agricultural products;

(4) stock minding, rearing and fattening;

(5) hiring out, for agricultural purposes, of equipment normally used in agricultural, forestry or fisheries undertakings;

(6) technical assistance;

(7) destruction of weeds and pests, dusting and spraying of crops and land;

(8) operation of irrigation and drainage equipment;

(9) lopping, tree felling and other forestry services.

Annex IX

Works of Art, Collectors' Items and Antiques, as referred to in points (2), (3) and (4) of article 311(1)

PART A: Works of art

(1) Pictures, collages and similar decorative plaques, paintings and drawings, executed entirely by hand by the artist, other than plans and drawings for architectural, engineering, industrial, commercial, topographical or similar purposes, hand-decorated manufactured articles, theatrical scenery, studio back cloths or the like of painted canvas (CN code 9701);

(2) original engravings, prints and lithographs, being impressions produced in limited numbers directly in black and white or in color of one or of several plates executed entirely by hand by the artist, irrespective of the process or of the material employed, but not including any mechanical or photomechanical process (CN code 97020000);

(3) original sculptures and statuary, in any material, provided that they are executed entirely by the artist; sculpture casts the production of which is limited to eight copies and supervised by the artist or his successors in title (CN code 97030000); on an exceptional basis, in cases determined by the Member States, the limit of eight copies may be exceeded for statuary casts produced before 1 January 1989;

(4) tapestries (CN code 58050000) and wall textiles (CN code 63040000) made by hand from original designs provided by artists, provided that there are not more than eight copies of each;

(5) individual pieces of ceramics executed entirely by the artist and signed by him;

(6) enamels on copper, executed entirely by hand, limited to eight numbered copies bearing the signature of the artist or the studio, excluding articles of jewellery and goldsmiths' and silversmiths' wares;

(7) photographs taken by the artist, printed by him or under his supervision, signed and numbered and limited to 30 copies, all sizes and mounts included.

PART B: Collectors' items

(1) Postage or revenue stamps, postmarks, first-day covers, pre-stamped stationery and the like, used, or if unused not current and not intended to be current (CN code 97040000);

(2) collections and collectors' pieces of zoological, botanical, mineralogical, anatomical, historical, archaeological, paleontological, ethnographic or numismatic interest (CN code 97050000).

PART C: Antiques

Goods, other than works of art or collectors' items, which are more than 100 years old (CN code 97060000).

Annex X

List of transactions covered by the derogations referred to in Articles 370 and 371 and Articles 375 to 390c

PART A: Transactions which Member States may continue to tax

(1) The supply of services by dental technicians in their professional capacity and the supply of dental prostheses by dentists and dental technicians;

(2) the activities of public radio and television bodies other than those of a commercial nature;

(3) the supply of a building, or parts thereof, or of the land on which it stands, other than as referred to in point (a) of Article 12(1), where carried out by taxable persons who were entitled to deduction of the VAT paid at the preceding stage in respect of the building concerned;

(4) the supply of the services of travel agents, as referred to in Article 306, and those of travel agents acting in the name and on behalf of the traveler, in relation to journeys outside the Community.

PART B: Transactions which Member States may continue to exempt

(1) Admission to sporting events;

(2) the supply of services by authors, artists, performers, lawyers and other members of the liberal professions, other than the medical and paramedical professions, with the exception of the following:

    (a) assignments of patents, trade marks and other similar rights, and the granting of licenses in respect of such rights;

    (b) work, other than the supply of contract work, on movable tangible property, carried out for a taxable person;

    (c) services to prepare or coordinate the carrying out of construction work, such as services provided by architects and by firms providing on-site supervision of works;

    (d) commercial advertising services;

    (e) transport and storage of goods, and ancillary services;

    (f) hiring out of movable tangible property to a taxable person;

    (g) provision of staff to a taxable person;

    (h) provision of services by consultants, engineers, planning offices and similar services in scientific, economic or technical fields;

    (i) compliance with an obligation to refrain from exercising, in whole or in part, a business activity or a right covered by points (a) to (h) or point (j);

(j) the services of forwarding agents, brokers, business agents and other independent intermediaries, in so far as they relate to the supply or importation of goods or the supply of services covered by points (a) to (i);

(3) the supply of telecommunications services, and of goods related thereto, by public postal services;

(4) the supply of services by undertakers and cremation services and the supply of goods related thereto;

(5) transactions carried out by blind persons or by workshops for the blind, provided that those exemptions do not cause significant distortion of competition;

(6) the supply of goods and services to official bodies responsible for the construction, setting out and maintenance of cemeteries, graves and monuments commemorating the war dead;

(7) transactions carried out by hospitals not covered by point (b) of Article 132(1);

(8) the supply of water by a body governed by public law;

(9) the supply before first occupation of a building, or parts thereof, or of the land on which it stands and the supply of building land, as referred to in Article 12;

(10) the transport of passengers and, in so far as the transport of the passengers is exempt, the transport of goods accompanying them, such as luggage or motor vehicles, or the supply of services relating to the transport of passengers;

(11) the supply, modification, repair, maintenance, chartering and hiring of aircraft used by State institutions, including equipment incorporated or used in such aircraft;

(12) the supply, modification, repair, maintenance, chartering and hiring of fighting ships;

(13) the supply of the services of travel agents, as referred to in Article 306, and those of travel agents acting in the name and on behalf of the traveler, in relation to journeys within the Community.

Annex XI

Repealed directives and time limits for transposition

Part A Repealed Directives with their successive amendments

(1)	Directive 67/227/EEC (OJ71, 14.4.1967, p.1301
(2)	Directive 77/388/EEC (Sixth Directive) (OJ L 145 of 13.6.1977, p. 1) Directive 78/583/EEC (OJ L 194 of 19.7.1978, p. 16) Directive 80/368/EEC (OJ L 90 of 3.4.1980, p. 41) Directive 84/386/EEC (OJ L 208 of 3.8.1984, p. 58) Directive 89/465/EEC (OJ L 226 of 3.8.1989, p. 21) Directive 91/680/EEC (OJ L 376 of 31.12.1991, p. 1) - (except for Article 2) Directive 92/77/EEC (OJ L 316 of 31.10.1992, p. 1) Directive 92/111/EEC (OJ L 384 of 30.12.1992, p. 47) Directive 94/4/EC (OJ L 60 of 3.3.1994, p. 14) - (only Article 2) Directive 94/5/EC (OJ L 60 of 3.3.1994, p. 16) Directive 94/76/EC (OJ L 365 of 31.12.1994, p. 53) Directive 95/7/EC (OJ L 102 of 5.5.1995, p. 18) Directive 96/42/EC (OJ L 170 of 9.7.1996, p. 34) Directive 96/95/EC (OJ L 338 of 28.12.1996, p. 89) Directive 98/80/EC (OJ L 281 of 17.10.1998, p. 31) Directive 1999/49/EC (OJ L 139 of 2.6.1999, p. 27) Directive 1999/59/EC (OJ L 162 of 26.6.1999, p. 63) Directive 1999/85/EC (OJ L 277 of 28.10.1999, p. 34) Directive 2000/17/EC (OJ L 84 of 5.4.2000, p. 24) Directive 2000/65/EC (OJ L 269 of 21.10.2000, p. 44) Directive 2001/4/EC (OJ L 22 of 24.1.2001, p. 17) Directive 2001/115/EC (OJ L 15 of 17.1.2001, p. 24) Directive 2002/38/EC (OJ L 128 of 15.5.2002, p. 41) Directive 2002/93/EC (OJ L 331 of 7.12.2002, p. 27) Directive 2003/92/EC (OJ L 260 of 11.10.2003, p. 8) Directive 2004/7/EC (OJ L 27 of 30.1.2004, p. 44) Directive 2004/15/EC (OJ L 52 of 21.2.2004, p. 61) Directive 2004/66/EC (OJ L 168 of 1.5.2004, p. 35) - (only Point V of the Annex) Directive 2005/92/EC (OJ L 345 of 28.12.2005, p. 19) Directive 2006/18/EC (OJ L 51 of 22.2.2006, p. 12) Directive 2006/58/EC (OJ L 174 of 28.6.2006, p. 5) Directive 2006/69/EC (OJ L 221 of 12.8.2006, p. 9) - (only Article 1) Directive 2006/98/EC (OJ L 363 of 20.12.2006, p. 129) - (only Point 2 of the Annex)

Part B Time limits for transposition into national law (referred to in Article 411)

Directive	Deadline for transposition
Directive 67/227/EEC	1 January 1970
Directive 77/388/EEC	1 January 1978
Directive 78/583/EEC	1 January 1979
Directive 80/368/EEC	1 January 1979
Directive 84/386/EEC	1 July 1985
Directive 89/465/EEC	1 January 1990 1 January 1991 1 January 1992 1 January 1993 1 January 1994 for Portugal
Directive 91/680/EEC	1 January 1993
Directive 92/77/EEC	31 December 1992
Directive 92/111/EEC	1 January 1993 1 January 1994 1 October 1993 for Germany
Directive 94/4/EC	1 April 1994
Directive 94/5/EC	1 January 1995
Directive 94/76/EC	1 January 1995
Directive 95/7/EC	1 January 1996 1 January 1997 for Germany and Luxembourg
Directive 96/42/EC	1 January 1995
Directive 96/95/EC	1 January 1997
Directive 98/80/EC	1 January 2000
Directive 1999/49/EC	1 January 1999
Directive 1999/59/EC	1 January 2000
Directive 1999/85/CE	—
Directive 2000/17/EC	—
Directive 2000/65/EC	31 December 2001
Directive 2001/4/EC	1 January 2001
Directive 2001/115/EC	1 January 2004
Directive 2002/38/EC	1 July 2003
Directive 2002/93/EC	—
Directive 2003/92/EC	1 January 2005
Directive 2004/7/EC	30 January 2004
Directive 2004/15/EC	—
Directive 2004/66/EC	1 May 2004
Directive 2005/92/EC	1 January 2006
Directive 2006/18/EC	—
Directive 2006/58/EC	1 July 2006
Directive 2006/69/EC	1 January 2008
Directive 2006/98/EC	1 January 2007

RECAST VAT DIRECTIVE

Annex XII

Correlation Table

Directive 67/227/EEC	Directive 77/388/EEC	Amending Directives	Other acts	This Directive
Article 1, first paragraph				Article 1(1)
Article 1, second and third paragraphs				—
Article 2, first, second and third paragraphs				Article 1(2), first, second and third subparagraphs
Articles 3, 4 and 6				—
	Article 1			—
	Article 2, point (1)			Article 2(1)(a) and (c)
	Article 2, point (2)			Article 2(1)(d)
	Article 3(1), first indent			Article 5, point (2)
	Article 3(1), second indent			Article 5, point (1)
	Article 3(1), third indent			Article 5, points (3) and (4)
	Article 3(2)			—
	Article 3(3), first subparagraph, first indent			Article 6(2)(a) and (b)
	Article 3(3), first subparagraph, second indent			Article 6(2)(c) and (d)
	Article 3(3), first subparagraph, third indent			Article 6(2)(e), (f) and (g)

Directive 67/227/EEC	Directive 77/388/EEC	Amending Directives	Other acts	This Directive
	Article 3(3) second subparagraph, first indent			Article 6(1)(b)
	Article 3(3) second subparagraph, second indent			Article 6(1)(c)
	Article 3(3), second subparagraph, third indent			Article 6(1)(a)
	Article 3(4), first subparagraph, first and second indents			Article 7(1)
	Article 3(4), second subparagraph, first, second and third indents			Article 7(2)
	Article 3(5)			Article 8
	Article 4(1) and (2)			Article 9(1), first and second subparagraphs
	Article 4(3)(a), first subparagraph, first sentence			Article 12(1)(a)
	Article 4(3)(a), first subparagraph, second sentence			Article 12(2), second subparagraph
	Article 4(3)(a), second subparagraph			Article 12(2), third subparagraph
	Article 4(3)(a), third subparagraph			Article 12(2), first subparagraph
	Article 4(3)(b), first subparagraph			Article 12(1)(b)
	Article 4(3)(b), second subparagraph			Article 12(3)

Directive 67/227/EEC	Directive 77/388/EEC	Amending Directives	Other acts	This Directive
	Article 6(2), first subparagraph, points (a) and (b)			Article 26(1)(a) and (b)
	Article 6(2), second subparagraph			Article 26(2)
	Article 6(3)			Article 27
	Article 6(4)			Article 28
	Article 6(5)			Article 29
	Article 7(1)(a) and (b)			Article 30, first and second paragraphs
	Article 7(2)			Article 60
	Article 7(3), first and second subparagraphs			Article 61, first and second paragraphs
	Article 8(1)(a), first sentence			Article 32, first paragraph
	Article 8(1)(a), second and third sentences			Article 36, first and second paragraphs
	Article 8(1)(b)			Article 31
	Article 8(1)(c), first subparagraph			Article 37(1)
	Article 8(1)(c), second subparagraph, first indent			Article 37(2), first subparagraph
	Article 8(1)(c), second subparagraph, second and third indents			Article 37(2), second and third subparagraphs
	Article 8(1)(c), third subparagraph			Article 37(2), fourth subparagraph

Directive 67/227/EEC	Directive 77/388/EEC	Amending Directives	Other acts	This Directive
	Article 8(1)(c), fourth subparagraph			Article 37(3), first subparagraph
	Article 8(1)(c), fifth subparagraph			—
	Article 8(1)(c), sixth subparagraph			Article 37(3), second subparagraph
	Article 8(1)(d), first and second subparagraphs			Article 38(1) and (2)
	Article 8(1)(e), first sentence			Article 39, first paragraph
	Article 8(1)(e), second and third sentences			Article 39, second paragraph
	Article 8(2)			Article 32, second paragraph
	Article 9(1)			Article 43
	Article 9(2) introductory sentence			—
	Article 9(2)(a)			Article 45
	Article 9(2)(b)			Article 46
	Article 9(2)(c), first and second indents			Article 52(a) and (b)
	Article 9(2)(c), third and fourth indents			Article 52(c)
	Article 9(2)(e), first to sixth indents			Article 56(1)(a) to (f)

RECAST VAT DIRECTIVE

Directive 67/227/EEC	Directive 77/388/EEC	Amending Directives	Other acts	This Directive
	Article 9(2)(e), seventh indent			Article 56(1)(f)
	Article 9(2)(e), eighth indent			Article 56(1)(g)
	Article 9(2)(e), ninth indent			Article 56(1)(h)
	Article 9(2)(e), tenth indent, first sentence			Article 56(1)(i)
	Article 9(2)(e), tenth indent, second sentence			Article 24(2)
	Article 9(2)(e), tenth indent, third sentence			Article 56(1)(i)
	Article 9(2)(e), eleventh and twelfth indents			Article 56(1)(j) and (k)
	Article 9(2)(f)			Article 57(1)
	Article 9(3)			Article 58, first and second paragraphs
	Article 9(3)(a) and (b)			Article 58, first paragraph, points (a) and (b)
	Article 9(4)			Article 59(1) and (2)
	Article 10(1)(a) and (b)			Article 62, points (1) and (2)
	Article 10(2), first subparagraph, first sentence			Article 63

Directive 67/227/EEC	Directive 77/388/EEC	Amending Directives	Other acts	This Directive
	Article 10(2), first subparagraph, second and third sentences			Article 64(1) and (2)
	Article 10(2), second subparagraph			Article 65
	Article 10(2), third subparagraph, first, second and third indents			Article 66(a), (b) and (c)
	Article 10(3), first subparagraph, first sentence			Article 70
	Article 10(3), first subparagraph, second sentence			Article 71(1), first subparagraph
	Article 10(3), second subparagraph			Article 71(1), second subparagraph
	Article 10(3), third subparagraph			Article 71(2)
	Article 11(A)(1)(a)			Article 73
	Article 11(A)(1)(b)			Article 74
	Article 11(A)(1)(c)			Article 75
	Article 11(A)(1)(d)			Article 77
	Article 11(A)(2)(a)			Article 78, first paragraph, point (a)
	Article 11(A)(2)(b), first sentence			Article 78, first paragraph, point (b)
	Article 11(A)(2)(b), second sentence			Article 78, second paragraph
	Article 11(A)(3)(a) and (b)			Article 79, first paragraph, points (a) and (b) Article 87(a) and (b)
	Article 11(A)(3)(c), first sentence			Article 79, first paragraph, point (c)

Directive 67/227/EEC	Directive 77/388/EEC	Amending Directives	Other acts	This Directive
	Article 11(A)(3)(c), second sentence			Article 79, second paragraph
	Article 11(A)(4), first and second subparagraphs			Article 81, first and second paragraphs
	Article 11(A)(5)			Article 82
	Article 11(A)(6), first subparagraph, first and second sentences			Article 80(1), first subparagraph
	Article 11(A)(6), first subparagraph, third sentence			Article 80(1), second subparagraph
	Article 11(A)(6), second subparagraph			Article 80(1), first subparagraph
	Article 11(A)(6), third subparagraph			--Article 80(2)
	Article 11(A)(6), fourth subparagraph			Article 80(3)
	Article 11(A)(7), first and second subparagraphs			Article 72, first and second paragraphs
	Article 11(B)(1)			Article 85
	Article 11(B)(3)(a)			Article 86(1)(a)
	Article 11(B)(3)(b), first subparagraph			Article 86(1)(b)
	Article 11(B)(3)(b), second subparagraph			Article 86(2)

Directive 67/227/EEC	Directive 77/388/EEC	Amending Directives	Other acts	This Directive
	Article 11(B)(3)(b), third subparagraph			Article 86(1)(b)
	Article 11(B)(4)			Article 87
	Article 11(B)(5)			Article 88
	Article 11(B)(6), first and second subparagraphs			Article 89, first and second paragraphs
	Article 11(C)(1), first and second subparagraphs			Article 90(1) and (2)
	Article 11(C)(2), first subparagraph			Article 91(1)
	Article 11(C)(2), second subparagraph, first and second sentences			Article 91(2), first and second subparagraphs
	Article 11(C)(3), first and second indents			Article 92(a) and (b)
	Article 12(1)			Article 93, first paragraph
	Article 12(1)(a)			Article 93, second paragraph, point (a)
	Article 12(1)(b)			Article 93, second paragraph, point (c)
	Article 12(2), first and second indents			Article 95, first and second paragraphs
	Article 12(3)(a), first subparagraph, first sentence			Article 96

RECAST VAT DIRECTIVE

Directive 67/227/EEC	Directive 77/388/EEC	Amending Directives	Other acts	This Directive
	Article 12(3)(a), first subparagraph, second sentence			Article 97(1)
	Article 12(3)(a), second subparagraph			Article 97(2)
	Article 12(3)(a), third subparagraph, first sentence			Article 98(1)
	Article 12(3)(a), third subparagraph, second sentence			Article 98(2), first subparagraph Article 99(1)
	Article 12(3)(a), fourth subparagraph			Article 98(2), second subparagraph
	Article 12(3)(b), first sentence			Article 102, first paragraph
	Article 12(3)(b), second, third and fourth sentences			Article 102, second paragraph
	Article 12(3)(c), first subparagraph			Article 103(1)
	Article 12(3)(c), second subparagraph, first and second indents			Article 103(2)(a) and (b)
	Article 12(4), first subparagraph			Article 99(2)
	Article 12(4), second subparagraph, first and second sentences			Article 100, first and second paragraphs
	Article 12(4), third subparagraph			Article 101
	Article 12(5)			Article 94(2)
	Article 12(6)			Article 105

Directive 67/227/EEC	Directive 77/388/EEC	Amending Directives	Other acts	This Directive
	Article 13(A)(1), introductory sentence			Article 131
	Article 13(A)(1)(a) to (n)			Article 132(1)(a) to (n)
	Article 13(A)(1)(o), first sentence			Article 132(1)(o)
	Article 13(A)(1)(o), second sentence			Article 132(2)
	Article 13(A)(1)(p) and (q)			Article 132(1)(p) and (q)
	Article 13(A)(2)(a), first to fourth indents			►C1 Article 133, first paragraph, points (a) to (d) ◄
	Article 13(A)(2)(b), first and second indents			Article 134(a) and (b)
	Article 13(B), introductory sentence			Article 131
	Article 13(B)(a)			Article 135(1)(a)
	Article 13(B)(b), first subparagraph			Article 135(1)(l)
	Article 13(B)(b), first subparagraph, points (1) to (4)			Article 135(2), first subparagraph, points (a) to (d)
	Article 13(B)(b), second subparagraph			Article 135(2), second subparagraph
	Article 13(B)(c)			Article 136(a) and (b)
	Article 13(B)(d)			—
	Article 13(B)(d), points (1) to (5)			Article 135(1)(b) to (f)

Directive 67/227/EEC	Directive 77/388/EEC	Amending Directives	Other acts	This Directive
	Article 13(B)(d), point (5), first and second indents			Article 135(1)(f)
	Article 13(B)(d), point (6)			Article 135(1)(g)
	Article 13(B)(e) to (h)			Article 135(1)(h) to (k)
	Article 13(C), first subparagraph, point (a)			Article 137(1)(d)
	Article 13(C), first subparagraph, point (b)			Article 137(1)(a), (b) and (c)
	Article 13(C), second subparagraph			Article 137(2), first and second subparagraphs
	Article 14(1), introductory sentence			Article 131
	Article 14(1)(a)			►C1 Article 143 (a) ◄
	Article 14(1)(d), first and second subparagraphs			Article 143(b) and (c)
	Article 14(1)(e)			Article 143(e)
	Article 14(1)(g), first to fourth indents			Article 143(f) to (i)
	Article 14(1)(h)			Article 143(j)
	Article 14(1)(i)			Article 144
	Article 14(1)(j)			Article 143(k)
	Article 14(1)(k)			Article 143(l)
	Article 14(2), first subparagraph			Article 145(1)

Directive 67/227/EEC	Directive 77/388/EEC	Amending Directives	Other acts	This Directive
	Article 14(2), second subparagraph, first, second and third indents			Article 145(2), first, second and third subparagraphs
	Article 14(2), third subparagraph			Article 145(3)
	Article 15, introductory sentence			Article 131
	Article 15, point (1)			Article 146(1)(a)
	Article 15, point (2), first subparagraph			Article 146(1)(b)
	Article 15, point (2), second subparagraph, first and second indents			Article 147(1), first subparagraph, points (a) and (b)
	Article 15, point (2), second subparagraph, third indent, first part of the sentence			Article 147(1), first subparagraph, point (c)
	Article 15, point (2), second subparagraph, third indent, second part of the sentence			Article 147(1), second subparagraph
	Article 15, point (2), third subparagraph, first and second indents			Article 147(2), first and second subparagraphs
	Article 15, point (2), fourth subparagraph			Article 147(2), third subparagraph
	Article 15, point (3)			Article 146(1)(d)
	Article 15, point (4), first subparagraph, points (a) and (b)			Article 148(a)
	Article 15, point (4), first subparagraph, point (c)			Article 148(b)
	Article 15, point (4), second subparagraph, first and second sentences			Article 150(1) and (2)
	Article 15, point (5)			Article 148(c)

RECAST VAT DIRECTIVE

Directive 67/227/EEC	Directive 77/388/EEC	Amending Directives	Other acts	This Directive
	Article 15, point (6)			Article 148(f)
	Article 15, point (7)			Article 148(e)
	Article 15, point (8)			Article 148(d)
	Article 15, point (9)			Article 148(g)
	Article 15, point (10), first subparagraph, first to fourth indents			Article 151(1), first subparagraph, points (a) to (d)
	Article 15, point (10), second subparagraph			Article 151(1), second subparagraph
	Article 15, point (10), third subparagraph			Article 151(2)
	Article 15, point (11)			Article 152
	Article 15, point (12), first sentence			Article 146(1)(c)
	Article 15, point (12), second sentence			Article 146(2)
	Article 15, point (13)			Article 146(1)(e)
	Article 15, point (14), first and second subparagraphs			Article 153, first and second paragraphs
	Article 15, point (15)			Article 149
	Article 16(1)			—
	Article 16(2)			Article 164(1)
	Article 16(3)			Article 166
	Article 17(1)			Article 167
	Article 17(2), (3) and (4)			—

Directive 67/227/EEC	Directive 77/388/EEC	Amending Directives	Other acts	This Directive
	Article 17(5), first and second subparagraphs			Article 173(1), first and second subparagraphs
	Article 17(5), third subparagraph, points (a) to (e)			Article 173(2)(a) to (e)
	Article 17(6)			Article 176
	Article 17(7), first and second sentences			Article 177, first and second paragraphs
	Article 18(1)			—
	Article 18(2), first and second subparagraphs			Article 179, first and second paragraphs
	Article 18(3)			Article 180
	Article 18(4), first and second subparagraphs			Article 183, first and second paragraphs
	Article 19(1), first subparagraph, first indent			Article 174(1), first subparagraph, point (a)
	Article 19(1), first subparagraph, second indent, first sentence			Article 174(1), first subparagraph, point (b)
	Article 19(1), first subparagraph, second indent, second sentence			Article 174(1), second subparagraph
	Article 19(1), second subparagraph			Article 175(1)
	Article 19(2), first sentence			Article 174(2)(a)
	Article 19(2), second sentence			Article 174(2)(a) and (b)

Directive 67/227/EEC	Directive 77/388/EEC	Amending Directives	Other acts	This Directive
	Article 19(2), third sentence			Article 174(3)
	Article 19(3), first subparagraph, first and second sentences			Article 175(2), first subparagraph
	Article 19(3), first subparagraph, third sentence			Article 175(2), second subparagraph
	Article 19(3), second subparagraph			Article 175(3)
	Article 20(1), introductory sentence			Article 186
	Article 20(1)(a)			Article 184
	Article 20(1)(b), first part of the first sentence			Article 185(1)
	Article 20(1)(b), second part of the first sentence			Article 185(2), first subparagraph
	Article 20(1)(b), second sentence			Article 185(2), second subparagraph
	Article 20(2), first subparagraph, first sentence			Article 187(1), first subparagraph
	Article 20(2), first subparagraph, second and third sentences			Article 187(2), first and second subparagraphs
	Article 20(2), second and third subparagraphs			Article 187(1), second and third subparagraphs
	Article 20(3), first subparagraph, first sentence			Article 188(1), first subparagraph
	Article 20(3), first subparagraph, second sentence			Article 188(1), second and third subparagraphs

Directive 67/227/EEC	Directive 77/388/EEC	Amending Directives	Other acts	This Directive
	Article 20(3), first subparagraph, third sentence			Article 188(2)
	Article 20(3), second subparagraph			Article 188(2)
	Article 20(4), first subparagraph, first to fourth indents			Article 189(a) to (d)
	Article 20(4), second subparagraph			Article 190
	Article 20(5)			Article 191
	Article 20(6)			Article 192
	Article 21			—
	Article 22			—
	Article 22a			Article 249
	Article 23, first paragraph			Article 211, first paragraph Article 260
	Article 23, second paragraph			Article 211, second paragraph
	Article 24(1)			Article 281
	►C1 Article 24(2), introductory sentence ◄			Article 292
	Article 24(2)(a), first subparagraph			Article 284(1)
	Article 24(2)(a), second and third subparagraphs			Article 284(2), first and second subparagraphs
	Article 24(2)(b), first and second sentences			Article 285, first and second paragraphs

RECAST VAT DIRECTIVE

Directive 67/227/EEC	Directive 77/388/EEC	Amending Directives	Other acts	This Directive
	Article 24(2)(c)			Article 286
	Article 24(3), first subparagraph			Article 282
	Article 24(3), second subparagraph, first sentence			Article 283(2)
	Article 24(3), second subparagraph, second sentence			Article 283(1)(a)
	Article 24(4), first subparagraph			Article 288, first paragraph, points (1) to (4)
	Article 24(4), second subparagraph			Article 288, second paragraph
	Article 24(5)			Article 289
	Article 24(6)			Article 290
	Article 24(7)			Article 291
	Article 24(8)(a), (b) and (c)			Article 293, points (1), (2) and (3)
	Article 24(9)			Article 294
	►C1 Article 24a, first paragraph, first to tenth indents ◄			Article 287, points (7) to (16)
	Article 24a, second paragraph			—
	Article 25(1)			Article 296(1)

Directive 67/227/EEC	Directive 77/388/EEC	Amending Directives	Other acts	This Directive
	Article 25(2), first to eighth indents			Article 295(1), points (1) to (8)
	Article 25(3), first subparagraph, first sentence			Article 297, first paragraph, first sentence and second paragraph
	Article 25(3), first subparagraph, second sentence			Article 298, first paragraph
	Article 25(3), first subparagraph, third sentence			Article 299
	Article 25(3), first subparagraph, fourth and fifth sentences			Article 298, second paragraph
	Article 25(3), second subparagraph			Article 297, first paragraph, second sentence
	Article 25(4), first subparagraph			Article 272(1), first subparagraph, point (e)
	Article 25(5) and (6)			—
	Article 25(7)			Article 304
	Article 25(8)			Article 301(2)
	Article 25(9)			Article 296(2)
	Article 25(10)			Article 296(3)
	Article 25(11) and (12)			—
	Article 26(1) first and second sentences			Article 306(1), first and second subparagraphs
	Article 26(1) third sentence			Article 306(2)

Directive 67/227/EEC	Directive 77/388/EEC	Amending Directives	Other acts	This Directive
	Article 26(2), first and second sentences			Article 307, first and second paragraphs
	Article 26(2), third sentence			Article 308
	Article 26(3), first and second sentences			Article 309, first and second paragraphs
	Article 26(4)			Article 310
	Article 26a(A)(a), first subparagraph			Article 311(1), point (2)
	Article 26a(A)(a), second subparagraph			Article 311(2)
	Article 26a(A)(b) and (c)			Article 311(1), points (3) and (4)
	Article 26a(A)(d)			Article 311(1), point (1)
	Article 26a(A)(e) and (f)			Article 311(1), points (5) and (6)
	Article 26a(A)(g), introductory sentence			Article 311(1), point (7)
	Article 26a(A)(g), first and second indents			Article 311(3)
	Article 26a(B)(1)			Article 313(1)
	Article 26a(B)(2)			Article 314
	►C1 Article 26a(B)(2), first to fourth indents ◄			Article 314(a) to (d)

Directive 67/227/EEC	Directive 77/388/EEC	Amending Directives	Other acts	This Directive
	Article 26a(B)(3), first subparagraph, first and second sentences			Article 315, first and second paragraphs
	Article 26a(B)(3), second subparagraph			Article 312
	Article 26a(B)(3), second subparagraph, first and second indents			Article 312, points (1) and (2)
	Article 26a(B)(4), first subparagraph			Article 316(1)
	Article 26a(B)(4), first subparagraph, points (a), (b) and (c)			Article 316(1)(a), (b) and (c)
	Article 26a(B)(4), second subparagraph			Article 316(2)
	Article 26a(B)(4), third subparagraph, first and second sentences			Article 317, first and second paragraphs
	Article 26a(B)(5)			Article 321
	Article 26a(B)(6)			Article 323
	Article 26a(B)(7)			Article 322
	Article 26a(B)(7)(a), (b) and (c)			Article 322(a), (b) and (c)
	Article 26a(B)(8)			Article 324
	Article 26a(B)(9)			Article 325
	Article 26a(B)(10), first and second subparagraphs			Article 318(1), first and second subparagraphs

RECAST VAT DIRECTIVE

Directive 67/227/EEC	Directive 77/388/EEC	Amending Directives	Other acts	This Directive
	Article 26a(B)(10), third subparagraph, first and second indents			Article 318(2)(a) and (b)
	Article 26a(B)(10), fourth subparagraph			Article 318(3)
	Article 26a(B)(11), first subparagraph			Article 319
	Article 26a(B)(11), second subparagraph, point (a)			Article 320(1), first subparagraph
	Article 26a(B)(11), second subparagraph, points (b) and (c)			Article 320(1), second subparagraph
	Article 26a(B)(11), third subparagraph			Article 320(2)
	Article 26a(C)(1), introductory sentence			Article 333(1) Article 334
	Article 26a(C)(1), first to fourth indents			Article 334(a) to (d)
	Article 26a(C)(2), first and second indents			Article 336(a) and (b)
	Article 26a(C)(3)			Article 337
	Article 26a(C)(4), first subparagraph, first, second and third indents			Article 339, first paragraph, points (a), (b) and (c)
	Article 26a(C)(4), second subparagraph			Article 339, second paragraph
	Article 26a(C)(5), first and second subparagraphs			Article 340(1), first and second subparagraphs

Directive 67/227/EEC	Directive 77/388/EEC	Amending Directives	Other acts	This Directive
	Article 26a(C)(5), third subparagraph			Article 340(2)
	Article 26a(C)(6), first subparagraph, first and second indents			Article 338, first paragraph, points (a) and (b)
	Article 26a(C)(6), second subparagraph			Article 338, second paragraph
	Article 26a(C)(7)			Article 335
	Article 26a(D), introductory sentence			—
	Article 26a(D)(a)			Article 313(2) Article 333(2)
	Article 26a(D)(b)			Article 4(a) and (c)
	Article 26a(D)(c)			Article 35 Article 139(3), first subparagraph
	Article 26b(A), first subparagraph, point (i), first sentence			Article 344(1), point (1)
	Article 26b(A), first subparagraph, point (i), second sentence			Article 344(2)
	Article 26b(A), first subparagraph, point (ii), first to fourth indents			Article 344(1), point (2)
	Article 26b(A), second subparagraph			Article 344(3)
	Article 26b(A), third subparagraph			Article 345
	Article 26b(B), first subparagraph			Article 346
	Article 26b(B), second subparagraph			Article 347

Directive 67/227/EEC	Directive 77/388/EEC	Amending Directives	Other acts	This Directive
	Article 26b(C), first subparagraph			Article 348
	Article 26b(C), second subparagraph, first and second sentences			Article 349(1) and (2)
	Article 26b(C), third subparagraph			Article 350
	Article 26b(C), fourth subparagraph			Article 351
	Article 26b(D)(1)(a), (b) and (c)			Article 354(a), (b) and (c)
	Article 26b(D)(2)			Article 355
	Article 26b(E), first and second subparagraphs			Article 356(1), first and second subparagraphs
	Article 26b(E), third and fourth subparagraphs			Article 356(2) and (3)
	Article 26b(F), first sentence			Article 198(2) and (3)
	Article 26b(F), second sentence			Articles 208 and 255
	Article 26b(G)(1), first subparagraph			Article 352
	Article 26b(G)(1), second subparagraph			—
	Article 26b(G)(2)(a)			Article 353
	Article 26b(G)(2)(b), first and second sentences			Article 198(1) and (3)
	Article 26c(A)(a) to (e)			Article 358, points (1) to (5)
	Article 26c(B)(1)			Article 359

Directive 67/227/EEC	Directive 77/388/EEC	Amending Directives	Other acts	This Directive
	Article 26c(B)(2), first subparagraph			Article 360
	Article 26c(B)(2), second subparagraph, first part of the first sentence			Article 361(1)
	Article 26c(B)(2), second subparagraph, second part of the first sentence			Article 361(1)(a) to (e)
	Article 26c(B)(2), second subparagraph, second sentence			Article 361(2)
	Article 26c(B)(3), first and second subparagraphs			Article 362
	Article 26c(B)(4)(a) to (d)			Article 363(a) to (d)
	Article 26c(B)(5), first subparagraph			Article 364
	Article 26c(B)(5), second subparagraph			Article 365
	Article 26c(B)(6), first sentence			Article 366(1), first subparagraph
	Article 26c(B)(6), second and third sentences			Article 366(1), second subparagraph
	Article 26c(B)(6), fourth sentence			Article 366(2)
	Article 26c(B)(7), first sentence			Article 367, first paragraph
	Article 26c(B)(7), second and third sentences			Article 367, second paragraph

RECAST VAT DIRECTIVE

Directive 67/227/EEC	Directive 77/388/EEC	Amending Directives	Other acts	This Directive
	Article 6(2), first subparagraph, points (a) and (b)			Article 26(1)(a) and (b)
	Article 6(2), second subparagraph			Article 26(2)
	Article 6(3)			Article 27
	Article 6(4)			Article 28
	Article 6(5)			Article 29
	Article 7(1)(a) and (b)			Article 30, first and second paragraphs
	Article 7(2)			Article 60
	Article 7(3), first and second subparagraphs			Article 61, first and second paragraphs
	Article 8(1)(a), first sentence			Article 32, first paragraph
	Article 8(1)(a), second and third sentences			Article 36, first and second paragraphs
	Article 8(1)(b)			Article 31
	Article 8(1)(c), first subparagraph			Article 37(1)
	Article 8(1)(c), second subparagraph, first indent			Article 37(2), first subparagraph
	Article 8(1)(c), second subparagraph, second and third indents			Article 37(2), second and third subparagraphs
	Article 8(1)(c), third subparagraph			Article 37(2), fourth subparagraph

Directive 67/227/EEC	Directive 77/388/EEC	Amending Directives	Other acts	This Directive
	Article 8(1)(c), fourth subparagraph			Article 37(3), first subparagraph
	Article 8(1)(c), fifth subparagraph			—
	Article 8(1)(c), sixth subparagraph			Article 37(3), second subparagraph
	Article 8(1)(d), first and second subparagraphs			Article 38(1) and (2)
	Article 8(1)(e), first sentence			Article 39, first paragraph
	Article 8(1)(e), second and third sentences			Article 39, second paragraph
	Article 8(2)			Article 32, second paragraph
	Article 9(1)			Article 43
	Article 9(2) introductory sentence			—
	Article 9(2)(a)			Article 45
	Article 9(2)(b)			Article 46
	Article 9(2)(c), first and second indents			Article 52(a) and (b)
	Article 9(2)(c), third and fourth indents			Article 52(c)
	Article 9(2)(e), first to sixth indents			Article 56(1)(a) to (f)

Directive 67/227/EEC	Directive 77/388/EEC	Amending Directives	Other acts	This Directive
	Article 28(2)(a), third subparagraph, second and third sentences			Article 112, second paragraph
	Article 28(2)(b)			Article 113
	Article 28(2)(c), first and second sentences			Article 114(1), first and second subparagraphs
	Article 28(2)(c), third sentence			Article 114(2)
	Article 28(2)(d)			Article 115
	Article 28(2)(e), first and second subparagraphs			Article 118, first and second paragraphs
	Article 28(2)(f)			Article 120
	Article 28(2)(g)			—
	Article 28(2)(h), first and second subparagraphs			Article 121, first and second paragraphs
	Article 28(2)(i)			Article 122
	Article 28(2)(j)			Article 117(2)
	Article 28(2)(k)			Article 116
	Article 28(3)(a)			Article 370
	Article 28(3)(b)			Article 371
	Article 28(3)(c)			Article 391
	Article 28(3)(d)			Article 372

Directive 67/227/EEC	Directive 77/388/EEC	Amending Directives	Other acts	This Directive
	Article 28(3)(e)			Article 373
	Article 28(3)(f)			Article 392
	Article 28(3)(g)			Article 374
	Article 28(3a)			Article 376
	Article 28(4) and (5)			Article 393(1) and (2)
	Article 28(6), first subparagraph, first sentence			Article 106, first and second paragraphs
	Article 28(6), first subparagraph, second sentence			Article 106, third paragraph
	Article 28(6), second subparagraph, points (a), (b) and (c)			Article 107, first paragraph, points (a), (b) and (c)
	Article 28(6), second subparagraph, point (d)			Article 107, second paragraph
	Article 28(6), third subparagraph			Article 107, second paragraph
	Article 28(6), fourth subparagraph, points (a), (b) and (c)			Article 108(a), (b) and (c)
	Article 28(6), fifth and sixth subparagraphs			—
	Article 28a(1), introductory sentence			Article 2(1)
	Article 28a(1)(a), first subparagraph			Article 2(1)(b)(i)

RECAST VAT DIRECTIVE

Directive 67/227/EEC	Directive 77/388/EEC	Amending Directives	Other acts	This Directive
	Article 28a(1)(a), second subparagraph			Article 3(1)
	Article 28a(1)(a), third subparagraph			Article 3(3)
	Article 28a(1)(b)			Article 2(1)(b)(ii)
	Article 28a(1)(c)			Article 2(1)(b)(iii)
	Article 28a(1a)(a)			Article 3(1)(a)
	Article 28a(1a)(b), first subparagraph, first indent			Article 3(1)(b)
	Article 28a(1a)(b), first subparagraph, second and third indents			Article 3(2), first subparagraph, points (a) and (b)
	Article 28a(1a)(b), second subparagraph			Article 3(2), second subparagraph
	Article 28a(2), introductory sentence			—
	Article 28a(2)(a)			Article 2(2), point (a) (i), (ii), and (iii)
	Article 28a(2)(b), first subparagraph			Article 2(2), point (b)
	Article 28a(2)(b), first subparagraph, first and second indents			Article 2(2), point (b) (i), (ii), and (iii)
	Article 28a(2)(b), second subparagraph			Article 2(2), point (c)

Directive 67/227/EEC	Directive 77/388/EEC	Amending Directives	Other acts	This Directive
	Article 28a(3), first and second subparagraphs			Article 20, first and second paragraphs
	Article 28a(4), first subparagraph			Article 9(2)
	Article 28a(4), second subparagraph, first indent			Article 172(1), second subparagraph
	Article 28a(4), second subparagraph, second indent			Article 172(1), first subparagraph
	Article 28a(4), third subparagraph			Article 172(2)
	Article 28a(5)(b), first subparagraph			Article 17(1), first subparagraph
	Article 28a(5)(b), second subparagraph			Article 17(1), second subparagraph and (2), introductory sentence
	Article 28a(5)(b), second subparagraph, first indent			Article 17(2)(a) and (b)
	Article 28a(5)(b), second subparagraph, second indent			Article 17(2)(c)
	Article 28a(5)(b), second subparagraph, third indent			Article 17(2)(e)
	Article 28a(5)(b), second subparagraph, fifth, sixth and seventh indents			Article 17(2)(f), (g) and (h)
	Article 28a(5)(b), second subparagraph, eighth indent			Article 17(2)(d)
	Article 28a(5)(b), third subparagraph			Article 17(3)

Directive 67/227/EEC	Directive 77/388/EEC	Amending Directives	Other acts	This Directive
	Article 28a(6), first subparagraph			Article 21
	Article 28a(6), second subparagraph			Article 22
	Article 28a(7)			Article 23
	Article 28b(A)(1)			Article 40
	Article 28b(A)(2), first and second subparagraphs			Article 41, first and second paragraphs
	Article 28b(A)(2), third subparagraph, first and second indents			Article 42(a) and (b)
	Article 28b(B)(1), first subparagraph, first and second indents			Article 33(1)(a) and (b)
	Article 28b(B)(1), second subparagraph			Article 33(2)
	Article 28b(B)(2), first subparagraph			Article 34(1)(a)
	Article 28b(B)(2), first subparagraph, first and second indents			Article 34(1)(b) and (c)
	Article 28b(B)(2), second subparagraph, first and second sentences			Article 34(2), first and second subparagraphs
	Article 28b(B)(2), third subparagraph, first sentence			Article 34(3)
	Article 28b(B)(2), third subparagraph, second and third sentences			—
	Article 28b(B)(3), first and second subparagraphs			Article 34(4), first and second subparagraphs

Directive 67/227/EEC	Directive 77/388/EEC	Amending Directives	Other acts	This Directive
	Article 28b(C)(1), first indent, first subparagraph			Article 48, first paragraph
	Article 28b(C)(1), first indent, second subparagraph			Article 49
	Article 28b(C)(1), second and third indents			Article 48, second and third paragraphs
	Article 28b(C)(2) and (3)			Article 47, first and second paragraphs
	Article 28b(C)(4)			Article 51
	Article 28b(D)			Article 53
	Article 28b(E)(1), first and second subparagraphs			Article 50, first and second paragraphs
	Article 28b(E)(2), first and second subparagraphs			Article 54, first and second paragraphs
	Article 28b(E)(3), first and second subparagraphs			Article 44, first and second paragraphs
	Article 28b(F), first and second paragraphs			Article 55, first and second paragraphs
	Article 28c(A), introductory sentence			Article 131
	Article 28c(A)(a), first subparagraph			Article 138(1)
	Article 28c(A)(a), second subparagraph			Article 139(1), first and second subparagraphs
	Article 28c(A)(b)			Article 138(2)(a)

RECAST VAT DIRECTIVE

Directive 67/227/EEC	Directive 77/388/EEC	Amending Directives	Other acts	This Directive
	Article 28c(A)(c), first subparagraph			Article 138(2)(b)
	Article 28c(A)(c), second subparagraph			Article 139(2)
	Article 28c(A)(d)			Article 138(2)(c)
	Article 28c(B), introductory sentence			Articles 131
	Article 28c(B)(a), (b) and (c)			Article 140(a), (b) and (c)
	Article 28c(C)			Article 142
	Article 28c(D), first subparagraph			Article 143(d)
	Article 28c(D), second subparagraph			Article 131
	Article 28c(E), point (1), first indent, replacing Article 16(1)			
	— paragraph 1, first subparagraph			Article 155
	— paragraph 1, first subparagraph, point (A)			Article 157(1)(a)
	— paragraph 1, first subparagraph, point (B), first subparagraph, points (a), (b) and (c)			Article 156(1)(a), (b) and (c)
	— paragraph 1, first subparagraph, point (B), first subparagraph, point (d), first and second indents			Article 156(1)(d) and (e)
	— paragraph 1, first subparagraph, point (B), first subparagraph, point (e), first subparagraph			Article 157(1)(b)

Directive 67/227/EEC	Directive 77/388/EEC	Amending Directives	Other acts	This Directive
	— paragraph 1, first subparagraph, point (B), first subparagraph, point (e), second subparagraph, first indent			Article 154
	— paragraph 1, first subparagraph, point (B), first subparagraph, point (e), second subparagraph, second indent, first sentence			Article 154
	— paragraph 1, first subparagraph, point (B), first subparagraph, point (e), second subparagraph, second indent, second sentence			Article 157(2)
	— paragraph 1, first subparagraph, point (B), first subparagraph, point (e), third subparagraph, first indent			—
	— paragraph 1, first subparagraph, point (B), first subparagraph, point (e), third subparagraph, second, third and fourth indents			Article 158(1)(a), (b) and (c)
	— paragraph 1, first subparagraph, point (B), second subparagraph			Article 156(2)
	— paragraph 1, first subparagraph, point (C)			Article 159
	— paragraph 1, first subparagraph, point (D), first subparagraph, points (a) and (b)			Article 160(1)(a) and (b)
	— paragraph 1, first subparagraph, point (D), second subparagraph			Articles 160(2)
	— paragraph 1, first subparagraph, point (E), first and second indents			Article 161(a) and (b)
	— paragraph 1, second subparagraph			Article 202
	— paragraph 1, third subparagraph			Article 163

Directive 67/227/EEC	Directive 77/388/EEC	Amending Directives	Other acts	This Directive
	Article 28c(E), point (1), second indent, inserting paragraph 1a into Article 16			
	— paragraph 1a			Article 162
	Article 28c(E), point (2), first indent, amending Article 16(2)			
	— paragraph 2, first subparagraph			Article 164(1)
	Article 28c(E), point (2), second indent, inserting the second and third subparagraphs into Article 16(2)			
	— paragraph 2, second subparagraph			Article 164(2)
	— paragraph 2, third subparagraph			Article 165
	Article 28c(E), point (3), first to fifth indents			Article 141(a) to (e)
	Article 28d(1), first and second sentences			Article 68, first and second paragraphs
	Article 28d(2) and (3)			Article 69(1) and (2)
	Article 28d(4), first and second subparagraphs			Article 67(1) and (2)
	Article 28e(1), first subparagraph			Article 83
	Article 28e(1), second subparagraph, first and second sentences			Article 84(1) and (2)
	Article 28e(2)			Article 76
Directive 67/227/EEC	Directive 77/388/EEC	Amending Directives	Other acts	This Directive
	Article 28e(3)			Article 93, second paragraph, point (b)
	Article 28e(4)			Article 94(1)
	Article 28f, point (1) replacing Article 17(2), (3) and (4)			
	— paragraph 2(a)			Article 168(a)
	— paragraph 2(b)			Article 168(e)
	— paragraph 2(c)			Article 168(b) and (d)
	— paragraph 2(d)			Article 168(c)
	— paragraph 3(a), (b) and (c)			Article 169(a), (b) and (c) Article 170(a) and (b)
	— paragraph 4, first subparagraph, first indent			Article 171(1), first subparagraph
	— paragraph 4, first subparagraph, second indent			Article 171(2), first subparagraph
	— paragraph 4, second subparagraph, point (a)			Article 171(1), second subparagraph
	— paragraph 4, second subparagraph, point (b)			Article 171(2), second subparagraph
	— paragraph 4, second subparagraph, point (c)			Article 171(3)
	Article 28f, point (2) replacing Article 18(1)			
	— paragraph 1(a)			Article 178(a)
	— paragraph 1(b)			Article 178(e)

RECAST VAT DIRECTIVE

Directive 67/227/EEC	Directive 77/388/EEC	Amending Directives	Other acts	This Directive
	— paragraph 1(c)			Article 178(b) and (d)
	— paragraph 1(d)			Article 178(f)
	— paragraph 1(e)			Article 178(c)
	Article 28f, point (3) inserting paragraph 3a into Article 18			
	— paragraph 3a, first part of the sentence			Article 181
	— paragraph 3a, second part of the sentence			Article 182
	Article 28g replacing Article 21			
	— paragraph 1(a), first subparagraph			Article 193
	— paragraph 1(a), second subparagraph			Article 194(1) and (2)
	— paragraph 1(b)			Article 196
	— paragraph 1(c), first subparagraph, first, second and third indents			Article 197(1)(a), (b) and (c)
	— paragraph 1(c), second subparagraph			Article 197(2)
	— paragraph 1(d)			Article 203
	— paragraph 1(e)			Article 200
	— paragraph 1(f)			Article 195
	— paragraph 2			—
	— paragraph 2(a), first sentence			Article 204(1), first subparagraph

Directive 67/227/EEC	Directive 77/388/EEC	Amending Directives	Other acts	This Directive
	— paragraph 2(a), second sentence			Article 204(2)
	— paragraph 2(b)			Article 204(1), second subparagraph
	— paragraph 2(c), first subparagraph			Article 199(1)(a) to (g)
	— paragraph 2(c), second, third and fourth subparagraphs			Article 199(2), (3) and (4)
	— paragraph 3			Article 205
	— paragraph 4			Article 201
	Article 28h replacing Article 22			
	— paragraph 1(a), first and second sentences			Article 213(1), first and second subparagraphs
	— paragraph 1(b)			Article 213(2)
	— paragraph 1(c), first indent, first sentence			Article 214(1)(a)
	— paragraph 1(c), first indent, second sentence			Article 214(2)
	— paragraph 1(c), second and third indents			Article 214(1)(b) and (c)
	— paragraph 1(d), first and second sentences			Article 215, first and second paragraphs
	— paragraph 1(e)			Article 216
	— paragraph 2(a)			Article 242

Directive 67/227/EEC	Directive 77/388/EEC	Amending Directives	Other acts	This Directive
—	►C1 paragraph 2(b), first and second subparagraphs ◄			Article 243(1) and (2)
—	paragraph 3(a), first subparagraph, first sentence			Article 220, point (1)
—	paragraph 3(a), first subparagraph, second sentence			Article 220, points (2) and (3)
—	paragraph 3(a), second subparagraph			Article 220, points (4) and (5)
—	paragraph 3(a), third subparagraph, first and second sentences			Article 221(1), first and second subparagraphs
—	paragraph 3(a), fourth subparagraph			Article 221(2)
—	paragraph 3(a), fifth subparagraph, first sentence			Article 219
—	paragraph 3(a), fifth subparagraph, second sentence			Article 228
—	paragraph 3(a), sixth subparagraph			Article 222
—	paragraph 3(a), seventh subparagraph			Article 223
—	paragraph 3(a), eighth subparagraph, first and second sentences			Article 224(1) and (2)
—	paragraph 3(a), ninth subparagraph, first and second sentences			Article 224(3), first subparagraph
—	paragraph 3(a), ninth subparagraph, third sentence			Article 224(3), second subparagraph
—	paragraph 3(a), tenth subparagraph			Article 225

Directive 67/227/EEC	Directive 77/388/EEC	Amending Directives	Other acts	This Directive
—	paragraph 3(b), first subparagraph, first to twelfth indents			Article 226, points (1) to (12)
—	paragraph 3(b), first subparagraph, thirteenth indent			Article 226, points (13) and (14)
—	paragraph 3(b), first subparagraph, fourteenth indent			Article 226, point (15)
—	paragraph 3(b), second subparagraph			Article 227
—	paragraph 3(b), third subparagraph			Article 229
—	paragraph 3(b), fourth subparagraph			Article 230
—	paragraph 3(b), fifth subparagraph			Article 231
—	paragraph 3(c), first subparagraph			Article 232
—	paragraph 3(c), second subparagraph, introductory sentence			Article 233(1), first subparagraph
—	paragraph 3(c), second subparagraph, first indent, first sentence			Article 233(1), first subparagraph, point (a)
—	paragraph 3(c), second subparagraph, first indent, second sentence			Article 233(2)
—	paragraph 3(c), second subparagraph, second indent, first sentence			Article 233(1), first subparagraph, point (b)
—	paragraph 3(c), second subparagraph, second indent, second sentence			Article 233(3)
—	paragraph 3(c), third subparagraph, first sentence			Article 233(1), second subparagraph

RECAST VAT DIRECTIVE

Directive 67/227/EEC	Directive 77/388/EEC	Amending Directives	Other acts	This Directive
	— paragraph 3(c), third subparagraph, second sentence			Article 237
	— paragraph 3(c), fourth subparagraph, first and second sentences			Article 234
	— paragraph 3(c), fifth subparagraph			Article 235
	— paragraph 3(c), sixth subparagraph			Article 236
	— paragraph 3(d), first subparagraph			Article 244
	— paragraph 3(d), second subparagraph, first sentence			Article 245(1)
	— paragraph 3(d), second subparagraph, second and third sentences			Article 245(2), first and second subparagraphs
	— paragraph 3(d), third subparagraph, first and second sentences			Article 246, first and second paragraphs
	— paragraph 3(d), fourth, fifth and sixth subparagraphs			Article 247(1), (2) and (3)
	— paragraph 3(d), seventh subparagraph			Article 248
	— paragraph 3(e), first subparagraph			Articles 217 and 241
	— paragraph 3(e), second subparagraph			Article 218
	— paragraph 4(a), first and second sentences			Article 252(1)
	— paragraph 4(a), third and fourth sentences			Article 252(2), first and second subparagraphs
	— paragraph 4(a), fifth sentence			Article 250(2)

Directive 67/227/EEC	Directive 77/388/EEC	Amending Directives	Other acts	This Directive
	— paragraph 4(b)			Article 250(1)
	— paragraph 4(c), first indent, first and second subparagraphs			Article 251(a) and (b)
	— paragraph 4(c), second indent, first subparagraph			Article 251(c)
	— paragraph 4(c), second indent, second subparagraph			Article 251(d) and (e)
	— paragraph 5			Article 206
	— paragraph 6(a), first and second sentences			Article 261(1)
	— paragraph 6(a), third sentence			Article 261(2)
	— paragraph 6(b), first subparagraph			Article 262
	— paragraph 6(b), second subparagraph, first sentence			Article 263(1), first subparagraph
	— paragraph 6(b), second subparagraph, second sentence			Article 263(2)
	— paragraph 6(b), third subparagraph, first and second indents			Article 264(1)(a) and (b)
	— paragraph 6(b), third subparagraph, third indent, first sentence			Article 264(1)(d)
	— paragraph 6(b), third subparagraph, third indent, second sentence			Article 264(2), first subparagraph
	— paragraph 6(b), fourth subparagraph, first indent			Article 264(1)(c) and (e)

Directive 67/227/EEC	Directive 77/388/EEC	Amending Directives	Other acts	This Directive
	— paragraph 6(b), fourth subparagraph, second indent, first sentence			Article 264(1)(f)
	— paragraph 6(b), fourth subparagraph, second indent, second sentence			Article 264(2), second subparagraph
	— paragraph 6(b), fifth subparagraph, first and second indents			Article 265(1)(a) and (b)
	— paragraph 6(b), fifth subparagraph, third indent, first sentence			Article 265(1)(c)
	— paragraph 6(b), fifth subparagraph, third indent, second sentence			Article 265(2)
	— paragraph 6(c), first indent			Article 263(1), second subparagraph
	— paragraph 6(c), second indent			Article 266
	— paragraph 6(d)			Article 254
	— paragraph 6(e), first subparagraph			Article 268
	— paragraph 6(e), second subparagraph			Article 259
	— paragraph 7, first part of the sentence			Article 207, first paragraph Article 256 Article 267
	— paragraph 7, second part of the sentence			Article 207, second paragraph
	— paragraph 8, first and second subparagraphs			Article 273, first and second paragraphs
	— paragraph 9(a), first subparagraph, first indent			Article 272(1), first subparagraph, point (c)

Directive 67/227/EEC	Directive 77/388/EEC	Amending Directives	Other acts	This Directive
	— paragraph 9(a), first subparagraph, second indent			Article 272(1), first subparagraph, points (a) and (d)
	— paragraph 9(a), first subparagraph, third indent			Article 272(1), first subparagraph, point (b)
	— paragraph 9(a), second subparagraph			Article 272(1), second subparagraph
	— paragraph 9(b)			Article 272(3)
	— paragraph 9(c)			Article 212
	— paragraph 9(d), first subparagraph, first and second indents			Article 238(1)(a) and (b)
	— paragraph 9(d), second subparagraph, first to fourth indents			Article 238(2)(a) to (d)
	— paragraph 9(d), third subparagraph			Article 238(3)
	— paragraph 9(e), first subparagraph			Article 239
	— paragraph 9(e), second subparagraph, first and second indents			Article 240, points (1) and (2)
	— paragraph 10			Articles 209 and 257
	— paragraph 11			Articles 210 and 258
	— paragraph 12, introductory sentence			Article 269
	— paragraph 12(a), first, second and third indents			Article 270(a), (b) and (c)
	— paragraph 12(b), first, second and third indents			Article 271(a), (b) and (c)

RECAST VAT DIRECTIVE

Directive 67/227/EEC	Directive 77/388/EEC	Amending Directives	Other acts	This Directive
	Article 28i inserting a third subparagraph into Article 24(3)			
	— paragraph 3, third subparagraph			Article 283(1)(b) and (c)
	Article 28j, point (1) inserting a second subparagraph into Article 25(4)			
	— paragraph 4, second subparagraph			Article 272(2)
	Article 28j, point (2) replacing Article 25(5) and (6)			
	— paragraph 5, first subparagraph, points (a), (b) and (c)			Article 300, points (1), (2) and (3)
	— paragraph 5, second subparagraph			Article 302
	— paragraph 6(a), first subparagraph, first sentence			Article 301(1)
	— paragraph 6(a), first subparagraph, second sentence			Article 303(1)
	— paragraph 6(a), second subparagraph, first, second and third indents			Article 303(2)(a), (b) and (c)
	— paragraph 6(a), third subparagraph			Article 303(3)
	— paragraph 6(b)			Article 301(1)
	Article 28j, point (3) inserting a second subparagraph into Article 25(9)			
	— paragraph 9, second subparagraph			Article 305

Directive 67/227/EEC	Directive 77/388/EEC	Amending Directives	Other acts	This Directive
	Article 28k, point (1), first subparagraph			—
	Article 28k, point (1), second subparagraph, point (a)			Article 158(3)
	Article 28k, point (1), second subparagraph, points (b) and (c)			—
	Article 28k, points (2), (3) and (4)			—
	Article 28k, point (5)			Article 158(2)
	Article 28l, first paragraph			—
	Article 28l, second and third paragraphs			Article 402(1) and (2)
	Article 28l, fourth paragraph			—
	Article 28m			Article 399, first paragraph
	Article 28n			—
	Article 28o(1), introductory sentence			Article 326, first paragraph
	Article 28o(1)(a), first sentence			Article 327(1) and (3)
	Article 28o(1)(a), second sentence			Article 327(2)
	Article 28o(1)(b)			Article 328
	Article 28o(1)(c), first, second and third indents			Article 329(a), (b) and (c)

Directive 67/227/EEC	Directive 77/388/EEC	Amending Directives	Other acts	This Directive
	Article 28o(1)(d), first and second subparagraphs			Article 330, first and second paragraph
	Article 28o(1)(e)			Article 332
	Article 28o(1)(f)			Article 331
	Article 28o(1)(g)			Article 4(b)
	Article 28o(1)(h)			Article 35 Article 139(3), second subparagraph
	Article 28o(2)			Article 326, second paragraph
	Article 28o(3)			Article 341
	Article 28o(4)			—
	Article 28p(1), first, second and third indents			Article 405, points (1), (2) and (3)
	Article 28p(2)			Article 406
	Article 28p(3), first subparagraph, first and second indents			Article 407(a) and (b)
	Article 28p(3), second subparagraph			—
	Article 28p(4)(a) to (d)			Article 408(1)(a) to (d)
	Article 28p(5), first and second indents			Article 408(2)(a) and (b)

Directive 67/227/EEC	Directive 77/388/EEC	Amending Directives	Other acts	This Directive
	Article 28p(6)			Article 409
	Article 28p(7), first subparagraph, points (a), (b) and (c)			Article 410(1)(a), (b) and (c)
	Article 28p(7), second subparagraph, first indent			—
	►C1 Article 28p(7), second subparagraph, second and third indents ◄			►C1 Article 410(2)(a) and (b) ◄
	Article 29(1) to (4)			Article 398(1) to (4)
	Article 29a			Article 397
	Article 30(1)			Article 396(1)
	Article 30(2), first and second sentences			Article 396(2), first subparagraph
	Article 30(2), third sentence			Article 396(2), second subparagraph
	Article 30(3) and (4)			Article 396(3) and (4)
	Article 31(1)			—
	Article 31(2)			Article 400
	Article 33(1)			Article 401
	Article 33(2)			Article 2(3)
	Article 33a(1), introductory sentence			Article 274
	Article 33a(1)(a)			Article 275

RECAST VAT DIRECTIVE

Directive 67/227/EEC	Directive 77/388/EEC	Amending Directives	Other acts	This Directive
	Article 33a(1)(b)			Article 276
	Article 33a(1)(c)			Article 277
	Article 33a(2), introductory sentence			Article 278
	Article 33a(2)(a)			Article 279
	Article 33a(2)(b)			Article 280
	Article 34			Article 404
	Article 35			Article 403
	Articles 36 and 37			—
	Article 38			Article 414
	Annex A(I)(1) and (2)			Annex VII, point (1)(a) and (b)
	Annex A(I)(3)			Annex VII, points (1)(c) and (d)
	Annex A(II)(1) to (6)			Annex VII, points (2)(a) to (f)
	Annex A(III) and (IV)			Annex VII, points (3) and (4)
	Annex A(IV)(1) to (4)			Annex VII, points (4)(a) to (d)
	Annex A(V)			Article 295(2)
	Annex B, introductory sentence			Article 295(1), point (5)
	Annex B, first to ninth indents			Annex VIII, points (1) to (9)
	Annex C			—

Directive 67/227/EEC	Directive 77/388/EEC	Amending Directives	Other acts	This Directive
	Annex D(1) to (13)			Annex I, points (1) to (13)
	Annex E(2)			Annex X, Part A, point (1)
	Annex E(7)			Annex X, Part A, point (2)
	Annex E(11)			Annex X, Part A, point (3)
	Annex E(15)			Annex X, Part A, point (4)
	Annex F(1)			Annex X, Part B, point (1)
	Annex F(2)			Annex X, Part B, points (2)(a) to (j)
	Annex F(5) to (8)			Annex X, Part B, points (3) to (6)
	Annex F(10)			Annex X, Part B, point (7)
	Annex F(12)			Annex X, Part B, point (8)
	Annex F(16)			Annex X, Part B, point (9)
	Annex F(17), first and second subparagraphs			Annex X, Part B, point (10)
	Annex F(23)			Annex X, Part B, point (11)
	Annex F(25)			Annex X, Part B, point (12)
	Annex F(27)			Annex X, Part B, point (13)
	Annex G(1) and (2)			Article 391
	Annex H, first paragraph			Article 98(3)
	Annex H, second paragraph, introductory sentence			—
	Annex H, second paragraph, points (1) to (6)			Annex III, points (1) to (6)

Directive 67/227/EEC	Directive 77/388/EEC	Amending Directives	Other acts	This Directive
	Annex H, second paragraph, point (7), first and second subparagraphs			Annex III, points (7) and (8)
	Annex H, second paragraph, points (8) to (17)			Annex III, points (9) to (18)
	Annex I, introductory sentence			—
	Annex I(a), first to seventh indents			Annex IX, Part A, points (1) to (7)
	Annex I(b), first and second indents			Annex IX, Part B, points (1) and (2)
	Annex I(c)			Annex IX, Part C
	Annex J, introductory sentence			Annex V, introductory sentence
	Annex J			Annex V, points (1) to (25)
	Annex K(1), first, second and third indents			Annex IV, points (1)(a), (b) and (c)
	Annex K(2) to (5)			Annex IV, points (2) to (5)
	Annex L, first paragraph, points (1) to (5)			Annex II, points (1) to (5)
	Annex L, second paragraph			Article 56(2)
	Annex M, points (a) to (f)			Annex VI, points (1) to (6)
		Article 1, point (1), second subparagraph, of Directive 89/465/EEC		Article 133, second paragraph
		Article 2 of Directive 94/5/EC		Article 342
		Article 3, first and second sentences, of Directive 94/5/EC		Article 343, first and second paragraphs

Directive 67/227/EEC	Directive 77/388/EEC	Amending Directives	Other acts	This Directive
		Article 4 of Directive 2002/38/EC		Article 56(3) Article 57(2) Article 357
		Article 5 of Directive 2002/38/EC		—
			Annex VIII(II), point (2)(a) of the Act of Accession of Greece	Article 287, point (1)
			Annex VIII(II), point (2)(b) of the Act of Accession of Greece	Article 375
			Annex XXXII(IV), point (3)(a), first indent and second indent, first sentence, of the Act of Accession of Spain and Portugal	Article 287, points (2) and (3)
			Annex XXXII(IV), point (3)(b), first subparagraph, of the Act of Accession of Spain and Portugal	Article 377
			Annex XV(IX), point (2)(b), first subparagraph, of the Act of Accession of Austria, Finland and Sweden	Article 104
			Annex XV(IX), point (2)(c), first subparagraph, of the Act of Accession of Austria, Finland and Sweden	Article 287, point (4)

RECAST VAT DIRECTIVE

Directive 67/227/EEC	Directive 77/388/EEC	Amending Directives	Other acts	This Directive
			Annex XV(IX), point (2)(f), first subparagraph, of the Act of Accession of Austria, Finland and Sweden	Article 117(1)
			Annex XV(IX), point (2)(g), first subparagraph, of the Act of Accession of Austria, Finland and Sweden	Article 119
			Annex XV(IX), point (2)(h), first subparagraph, first and second indents, of the Act of Accession of Austria, Finland and Sweden	Article 378(1)
			Annex XV(IX), point (2)(i), first subparagraph, first indent, of the Act of Accession of Austria, Finland and Sweden	—
			Annex XV(IX), point (2)(i), first subparagraph, second and third indents, of the Act of Accession of Austria, Finland and Sweden	Article 378(2)(a) and (b)
			Annex XV(IX), point (2)(j) of the Act of Accession of Austria, Finland and Sweden	Article 287, point (5)
			Annex XV(IX), point (2)(l), first subparagraph, of the Act of Accession of Austria, Finland and Sweden	Article 111(a)

Directive 67/227/EEC	Directive 77/388/EEC	Amending Directives	Other acts	This Directive
			Annex XV(IX), point (2)(m), first subparagraph, of the Act of Accession of Austria, Finland and Sweden	Article 379(1)
			Annex XV(IX), point (2)(n), first subparagraph, first and second indents, of the Act of Accession of Austria, Finland and Sweden	Article 379(2)
			Annex XV(IX), point (2)(x), first indent, of the Act of Accession of Austria, Finland and Sweden	Article 253
			Annex XV(IX), point (2)(x), second indent, of the Act of Accession of Austria, Finland and Sweden	Article 287, point (6)
			Annex XV(IX), point (2)(r), first subparagraph, of the Act of Accession of Austria, Finland and Sweden	Article 111(b)
			Annex XV(IX), point (2)(aa), first subparagraph, first and second indents, of the Act of Accession of Austria, Finland and Sweden	Article 380
			Protocol No 2 of the Act of Accession of Austria, Finland and Sweden concerning the Åland Islands	Article 6(1)(d)

Directive 67/227/EEC	Directive 77/388/EEC	Amending Directives	Other acts	This Directive
			Annex V(5), point (1)(a) of the 2003 Act of Accession of the Czech Republic, Estonia, Cyprus, Latvia, Lithuania, Hungary, Malta, Poland Slovenia and Slovakia	Article 123
			Annex V(5), point (1)(b) of the 2003 Act of Accession	Article 381
			Annex VI(7), point (1)(a) of the 2003 Act of Accession	Article 124
			Annex VI(7), point (1)(b) of the 2003 Act of Accession	Article 382
			Annex VII(7), point (1), first and second subparagraphs, of the 2003 Act of Accession	Article 125(1) and (2)
			Annex VII(7), point (1), third subparagraph, of the 2003 Act of Accession	—
			Annex VII(7), point (1), fourth subparagraph, of the 2003 Act of Accession	Article 383(a)
			Annex VII(7), point (1), fifth subparagraph, of the 2003 Act of Accession	—

Directive 67/227/EEC	Directive 77/388/EEC	Amending Directives	Other acts	This Directive
			Annex VII(7), point (1), sixth subparagraph, of the 2003 Act of Accession	Article 383(b)
			Annex VIII(7), point (1)(a) of the 2003 Act of Accession	—
			Annex VIII(7), point (1)(b), second subparagraph, of the 2003 Act of Accession	Article 384(a)
			►C1 Annex VIII(7), point (1)(b), third subparagraph, of the 2003 Act of Accession ◄	Article 384(b)
			Annex IX(8), point (1) of the 2003 Act of Accession	Article 385
			Annex X(7), point (1)(a)(i) and (ii) of the 2003 Act of Accession	Article 126(a) and (b)
			Annex X(7), point (1)(c) of the 2003 Act of Accession	Article 386
			Annex XI(7), point (1) of the 2003 Act of Accession	Article 127
			Annex XI(7), point (2)(a) of the 2003 Act of Accession	Article 387(c)
			Annex XI(7), point (2)(b) of the 2003 Act of Accession	Article 387(a)

RECAST VAT DIRECTIVE

Directive 67/227/EEC	Directive 77/388/EEC	Amending Directives	Other acts	This Directive
			Annex XI(7), point (2)(c) of the 2003 Act of Accession	Article 387(b)
			Annex XII(9), point (1)(a) of the 2003 Act of Accession	Article 128(1) and (2)
			Annex XII(9), point (1)(b) of the 2003 Act of Accession	Article 128(3), (4) and (5)
			Annex XII(9), point (2) of the 2003 Act of Accession	Article 388
			Annex XIII(9), point (1)(a) of the 2003 Act of Accession	Article 129(1) and (2)
			Annex XIII(9), point (1)(b) of the 2003 Act of Accession	Article 389
			Annex XIV(7), first subparagraph, of the 2003 Act of Accession	Article 130(a) and (b)
			Annex XIV(7), second subparagraph, of the 2003 Act of Accession	—
			Annex XIV(7), third subparagraph, of the 2003 Act of Accession	Article 390

RECAST VAT DIRECTIVE

VAT e-Consultant app

VISIT US

AT

WWW.EASYGOTAX.COM

And test our VAT e-Consultant

www.ingramcontent.com/pod-product-compliance
Lightning Source LLC
Chambersburg PA
CBHW020905180526
45163CB00007B/2634